The God of All Comfort

HANNAH WHITALL SMITH

BARBOUR
PUBLISHING

Editorial assistance by Jill Jones.

Print ISBN 978-1-62029-763-6

eBook Editions:
Adobe Digital Edition (.epub) 978-1-62416-066-0
Kindle and MobiPocket Edition (.prc) 978-1-62416-065-3

Cover image: Alov/Veer Images

Published by Barbour Publishing, Inc., P.O. Box 719, Uhrichsville, Ohio 44683, www.barbourbooks.com

Our mission is to publish and distribute inspirational products offering exceptional value and biblical encouragement to the masses.

Member of the
Evangelical Christian
Publishers Association

Printed in the United States of America.

CONTENTS

Contents

Introduction

God isn't angry with you—He longs to give you peace and joy. That's the message of Hannah Whitall Smith's important and powerful book *The God of All Comfort.*

Now abridged and updated for today's reader, this late nineteenth-century study holds a well-deserved spot among the Christian classics, reminding God's children of His many promises of comfort, help, and love. Addressing God's powerful names, His role as shepherd and dwelling place, and His complete sufficiency for human needs, *The God of All Comfort* will show you that anxiety, fear, and insecurity are unnecessary feelings for Christians.

Born into a strict Quaker home in Pennsylvania in 1832, Hannah Whitall suffered from deep spiritual doubts during her early years. Her inner struggle continued into her marriage to Robert Piersall Smith in 1851, but in 1858 the couple committed their lives to Christ and decided to leave the Quaker faith to join the Plymouth Brethren.

A further spiritual experience in 1867 led Hannah and Robert to undertake a speaking tour on the "Higher Christian Life" in the United States and Europe. As Robert's health declined, the couple stayed in England and observed the 1874 founding of the Keswick Convention. It was at a Keswick conference in 1886 that Amy Carmichael would feel the call of God to the mission field.

Hannah Whitall Smith penned *The Christian's Secret of a Happy Life* in 1875 and wrote eighteen other books as well, including *The Unselfishness of God and How I Discovered It* in 1903.

Smith was stricken with arthritis for the last seven years of her life and was ultimately confined to a wheelchair, but she still entertained admirers of her writings. She died in 1911.

1

WHY THIS BOOK
HAS BEEN WRITTEN

My heart is overflowing with a good theme;
I recite my composition concerning the King.

PSALM 45:1

I was once talking on the subject of religion with an intelligent agnostic, whom I very much wished to influence, and after listening to me politely for a little while, he said, "Well, madam, all I have to say is this. If you Christians want to make us agnostics inclined to look into your religion, you must try to be more comfortable in the possession of it yourselves. The Christians I meet seem to me to be the most uncomfortable people around. They seem to carry their religion as a man carries a headache. He does not want to get rid of his head, but at the same time it is very uncomfortable to have it. And I for one do not care to have that sort of religion."

This was a lesson I have never forgotten, and it is the primary cause of my writing this book.

I was very young in the Christian life at the time of this conversation and was still in the first joy of my entrance into it, so I could not believe that any of God's children could be uncomfortable in their religious lives. But when the early glow of my conversion had passed and I had come down to the dullness of everyday duties and responsibilities, I soon found from my own experience, and also from the similar experiences of most of the Christians around me, that there was far too much truth in his assertion.

I confess that this was very disappointing, for I had expected something altogether different. It seemed to me incongruous that a religion whose fruits were declared in the

Bible to be love, joy, and peace should so often work out in an exactly opposite direction and should develop the fruits of doubt, fear, unrest, conflict, and discomforts of every kind. I resolved, if possible, to find out what was the matter. Why, I asked myself, should the children of God lead such utterly uncomfortable religious lives when He has led us to believe that His yoke would be easy and His burden light? Why are we tormented with so many spiritual doubts and such heavy spiritual anxieties? Why do we find it so hard to be sure that God really loves us? How is it that we can let ourselves suspect Him of forgetting us and forsaking us in times of need?

I believe I have found the answer to these questions, and I should like to state frankly that my object in writing this book is to try to bring into some troubled Christian lives around me a little real and genuine comfort.

A writer has said, "We know what over-advertisement is. It is a twentieth-century dis-ease from which we all suffer. There are posters on every billboard, exaggerations on every blank wall, representations and misrepresentations without number. Everything is overadvertised. Is it the same with the kingdom of God? Do the fruits that we raise from the good seed of the kingdom verify the description given by Him from whom we obtained that good seed? There is a feeling abroad that Christ has offered in His Gospel more than He has to give. People think that they have not exactly realized what was predicted as the portion of the children of God. But why is this so? Has the kingdom of God been overadvertised, or is it only that it has been underbelieved; has the Lord Jesus Christ been overestimated, or has He only been undertrusted?"

What I want to do in this book is to show what I firmly believe, that the kingdom of God could not possibly be overadvertised nor the Lord Jesus Christ overestimated, for "eye has not seen, nor ear heard, nor have entered into the heart of man the things which God has prepared for those who love Him" (1 Corinthians 2:9); and that all the difficulty arises from the fact that we have under-believed and undertrusted.

I want to show the grounds there are

in the religion of the Lord Jesus Christ for that deep and lasting peace and comfort of soul that nothing earthly can disturb. And I also want to tell, if this is indeed our rightful portion, how we are to avail ourselves of it and what hinders us. There is God's part in the matter, and there is man's part, and we must look carefully at both.

A wild young man who was brought to the Lord at a mission meeting and who became a rejoicing Christian and lived an exemplary life afterward was asked by someone what he did to get converted. "Oh," he said, "I did my part, and the Lord did His."

"But what was your part," asked the inquirer, "and what was the Lord's part?"

"My part," was the prompt reply, "was to run away, and the Lord's part was to run after me until He caught me."

God's part is always to run after us. Christ came to seek and to save that which is lost. " 'What man of you,' " He says, " 'having a hundred sheep, if he loses one of them, does not leave the ninety-nine in the wilderness, and go after the one which is lost until he finds it? And when he has found it, he lays it on his shoulders, rejoicing'" (Luke 15:4–5). This is always the divine part, but in our foolishness we do not understand it but think that the Lord is the one who is lost and that our part is to seek and find Him.

It is our ignorance of God that does it all. Because we do not know Him, we naturally get all sorts of wrong ideas about Him. We think He is an angry judge who is on the watch for our slightest faults, or a harsh taskmaster determined to exact from us the uttermost service, or a self-absorbed deity demanding His full measure of honor and glory, or a far-off sovereign concerned only with His own affairs and indifferent to our welfare. Who can wonder that such a God can neither be loved nor trusted?

But I can assert boldly that it is impossible for anyone who really knows God to have such thoughts about Him. Plenty of outward discomforts there may be, and many earthly sorrows and trials, but through them all the soul that knows God cannot but dwell inwardly in a fortress of perfect peace.

" 'Whoever listens to me,' " He says, " 'will dwell safely, and will be secure, without fear of evil' " (Proverbs 1:33). If we would really listen to God, we couldn't fail to know that, just because He is God, He can't do anything other than care for us as He cares for the apple of His eye. Not a single loophole for worry or fear is left to the soul that knows God.

"But how do I get to know Him?" you ask. "Other people seem to have some kind of inward revelation that makes them know Him, but I never do; and no matter how much I pray, everything seems dark. I want to know God, but I don't see how to manage it."

Your trouble is that you have a wrong idea of what knowing God is, or at least the kind of knowing I mean. I don't mean mystical revelations. Such revelations are delightful when you can have them, but they are not always at your command, and they are often variable and uncertain. The kind of knowing I mean is just the plain knowledge of God's nature and character that comes to us by believing what is revealed to us in the Bible concerning Him. The apostle John, at the close of his Gospel, says regarding the things he had been recording: "And truly Jesus did many other signs in the presence of His disciples, which are not written in this book; but these are written that you may believe that Jesus is the Christ, the Son of God, and that believing you may have life in His name" (John 20:30–31). It is believing the thing that is written, not the thing that is inwardly revealed, that is to give life; and the kind of knowing I mean is the knowing that comes from believing the things that are written.

When I read in the Bible that God is love, I am to believe it, just because "it is written." When the Bible says that He cares for us as He cares for the lilies of the field and the birds of the air, and that the very hairs of our head are all numbered, I am to believe it, just because it is written.

Inward revelations we cannot manage, but anyone in his senses can believe the thing that is written. And although this may seem very dry and bare to start with, it will, if steadfastly persevered in, result in very blessed inward revelations, and will sooner or later lead us into a knowledge of God that will transform our lives.

I will first try to show what God is in practical reality, and I will also point out some of the things that seem to me the principal hindrances to becoming really acquainted with Him.

I am so absolutely certain that coming to know Him as He really is will bring unfailing comfort and peace to every troubled heart that I long to help everyone within my reach to this knowledge. One of Job's friends said, in his arguments against Job's bitter complaints, "Now acquaint yourself with [God], and be at peace" (Job 22:21); and our Lord in His last recorded prayer said: "This is eternal life, that they may know You, the only true God, and Jesus Christ whom You have sent" (John 17:3). It is not a question of acquaintance with ourselves; it is simply a question of becoming acquainted with God and getting to know what He is and what He does and what He feels.

We may spend our days in what we call our religious duties and fill our devotions with fervor, and still be miserable. Nothing can set our hearts at rest but a real acquaintance with God, for everything in our salvation must depend on Him. If we were planning to take a dangerous voyage, our first question would be about the sort of captain we were to have. Our common sense would tell us that if the captain were untrustworthy, no amount of trustworthiness on our part would make the voyage safe, and it would be his character and not our own that would be the thing of paramount importance to us.

It must be clearly understood that my book does not propose to touch on the critical or the theological aspects of our religion. It does not undertake to deal with any questions concerning the authenticity of the Bible. Other and far abler minds can deal with these matters. My book is written for people who, like myself, profess to believe in the Lord Jesus Christ and who accept the Bible simply as the revelation of Him.

2

WHAT IS HIS NAME?

*Then Moses said to God, "Indeed, when I come to
the children of Israel and say to them, 'The God of
your fathers has sent me to you,' and they say to me,
'What is His name?' what shall I say to them?"*

EXODUS 3:13

The vital question of all ages and of every
human heart is here expressed: "What is His
name?"

The whole fate of humanity hangs on the
answer to this question.

The condition of a country depends on
the character of its rulers. The state of an
army depends on the officers who command

it. We can see how it must be, therefore, that everything in a universe will depend upon the sort of creator and ruler who has brought that universe into existence, and that the whole welfare of the human beings who have been placed there is bound up with the character of their Creator. If the God who created us is a good God, then everything must be all right for us, since a good God cannot ordain any but good things. But if He is a bad God or a careless God or an unkind God, then we cannot be sure that anything is right and can have no peace or comfort.

The true ground for peace and comfort is only to be found in the sort of God we have. Therefore, we need first of all to find out what is His name, or, in other words, what is His character.

In Bible language, name always means character. Names are not given arbitrarily there, as with us, but are always given with reference to the character or work of the person named. The names of God signify what He really is and are used throughout the Bible to express His attributes and His purposes, glory, grace, mercy, love, wisdom, power, and goodness.

When the children of Israel asked, "What is His name?" they meant, "Who and what is this God of whom you speak? What is His character; what are His attributes; what does He do? In short, what sort of a being is He?"

The psalmist says, "Those who know Your name will put their trust in You; for You, LORD, have not forsaken those who seek You" (Psalm 9:10). And in Proverbs we read, "The name of the LORD is a strong tower; the righteous run to it and are safe" (Proverbs 18:10). "Those who know Your name will put their trust in You." They cannot do anything else, because in knowing His name they know His character and His nature.

"Some trust in chariots, and some in horses; but we will remember the name of the LORD our God. They have bowed down and fallen; but we have risen and stand upright" (Psalm 20:7–8). In everything we read about Israel of old we find this constant refrain, that all they were and all they had depended upon the fact that their God was the Lord.

"Blessed is the nation whose God is the LORD, the people He has chosen as His own inheritance" (Psalm 33:12). "You are great, O Lord GOD. For there is none like You, nor is there any God besides You, according to all that we have heard with our ears. And who is like Your people, like Israel, the one nation on the earth whom God went to redeem for Himself as a people, to make for Himself a name—and to do for Yourself great and awesome deeds for Your land—before Your people whom You redeemed for Yourself from Egypt, the nations, and their gods? For You have made Your people Israel Your very own people forever; and You, LORD, have become their God" (2 Samuel 7:22–24). "Happy are the people whose God is the LORD!" (Psalm 144:15).

The question of all questions for each one of us, therefore, is this: "What is His name?" To the Israelites God Himself answered this question. "And God said to Moses, 'I AM WHO I AM.' And He said, 'Thus you shall say to the children of Israel, "I AM has sent me to you."'" Moreover God said to Moses:

'Thus you shall say to the children of Israel: "the LORD God of your fathers, the God of Abraham, the God of Isaac, and the God of Jacob, has sent me to you. This is My name forever, and this is My memorial to all generations"'" (Exodus 3:14–15).

In the Gospel of John, Christ adopts this name of "I am" as His own. When the Jews were questioning Him as to His authority, He said to them: "Most assuredly, I say to you, before Abraham was, I AM" (John 8:58). And in the book of Revelation He again declares: "'I am the Alpha and the Omega, the Beginning and the End,' says the Lord, 'who is and who was and who is to come, the Almighty'" (Revelation 1:8).

These simple words, *I am*, express eternity and unchangeableness, which is the very first element necessary in a God who is to be depended upon. No dependence could be placed by any one of us upon a changeable God. He must be the same yesterday, today, and forever if we are to have any peace or comfort.

But is this all His name implies, simply

"I am"? I am what? we ask. What does this "I am" include?

I believe it includes everything the human heart longs for and needs. This unfinished name of God seems to me like a blank check signed by a rich friend given to us to be filled in with whatever sum we may desire. The whole Bible tells us what it means.

Every attribute of God, every revelation of His character, every proof of His undying love, every declaration of His watchful care, every assertion of His purposes of tender mercy, every manifestation of His loving kindness—all are the filling out of this unfinished "I am."

God tells us through all the pages of His Book what He is. "I am," He says, "all that my people need": "I am their strength"; "I am their wisdom"; "I am their righteousness"; "I am their peace"; "I am their salvation"; "I am their life"; "I am their all in all."

This apparently unfinished name, therefore, is the most comforting name the heart of man could devise, because it allows us to add to it, without any limitation, whatever we feel the need of, and even "exceedingly abundantly" beyond all that we can ask or think.

But if our hearts are full of our own wretched "I ams" we will have no ears to hear His glorious, soul-satisfying "I am." We say, "I am so poor and weak," or "I am so foolish," or "I am a good-for-nothing," or "I am so helpless." We even feel that we should be pitied that things are so hard for us. All the time we are entirely ignoring the blank check of God's magnificent "I am," which authorizes us to draw upon Him for an abundant supply for every need.

What our Lord declares is eternally true: "I, if I am lifted up from the earth, will draw all peoples to Myself" (John 12:32). Once you know Him, Christ is absolutely irresistible. You can no more help trusting Him than you can help breathing.

How then can we become acquainted with God?

There are two things necessary: first, God must reveal Himself; and second, we must accept His revelation and believe what He reveals.

The apostle John tells us that "no one has seen God at any time," but "the only begotten Son, who is in the bosom of the Father, He has declared Him" (John 1:18). Christ, then, is the revelation of God. None of us have seen God, but He has incarnated Himself in Christ, and we can see Christ, since He was a man like one of us.

Christ revealed God by what He was, by what He did, and by what He said. From the cradle to the grave, every moment of His life was a revelation of God. We must go to Him then for our knowledge of God, and we must refuse to believe anything concerning God that is not revealed to us in Christ. Only in Christ do we see God as He is.

Just what God would have said and done under the circumstances, that's what Christ said and did. "I do nothing of Myself" (John 8:28) was His continual assertion. "The words that I speak to you I do not speak on My own authority; but the Father who dwells in Me does the works" (John 14:10); "I and My Father are one" (John 10:30); "he who sees Me sees Him who sent Me" (John 12:45).

Over and over we are assured that God and Christ are one. To His disciples He said: "'If you had known Me, you would have known My Father also; and from now on you know Him and have seen Him'" (John 14:7). But Philip couldn't understand this and said, "'Lord, show us the Father, and it is sufficient for us'" (John 14:8). And then Jesus repeated His former statement even more strongly: "'Have I been with you so long, and yet you have not known Me, Philip? He who has seen me has seen the Father; so how can you say, "Show us the Father"?'" (John 14:9).

We are all aware that the Old Testament revelation of God seems sometimes to contradict the revelation in Christ. In light of the fact that God Himself tells us that in these last days He has spoken to us by His Son, who is the "brightness of His glory and the express image of His person" (Hebrews 1:3), we don't dare reject Christ's testimony but must look upon the Old Testament revelation, where it differs from the revelation in Christ, as partial and imperfect, and must accept as a true representation of God only what we find in Christ. Christ alone tells us the true and genuine name of God. In His last wonderful prayer He says: "I have manifested Your name to the men whom You have given Me out of the world. They were Yours, You gave them to Me, and they have kept Your word. Now they have known that all things which You have given Me are from You. For I have given to them the words which You have given me; and they have received them, and have known surely that I came forth from You; and they have believed that You sent Me" (John 17:6–8).

Could we ask for greater authority than this?

The apostle declares most emphatically that it "pleased the Father" that in Christ "all the fullness should dwell" (Colossians 1:19). And although we may not understand all that this means theologically, we at least can't fail to see that if we want to know God, we just need to become acquainted with Christ's ways and character. He declares that "nor does anyone know the Father except the Son, and the one to whom the Son wills to reveal Him" (Matthew 11:27).

We may know a good many things about Him, but that is very different from knowing Him Himself, as He really is in nature and character. Other witnesses have told us of His visible acts, but from these we often get very wrong impressions of His true character. No other witness but Christ can tell us of the real secrets of God's heart, for of none other can it be said that "the only begotten Son, who is in the bosom of the Father, He has declared Him" (John 1:18). If we believe this to be a fact, then the stern judge and harsh taskmaster whom we have feared will disappear, and His place will be taken by the God of love.

If we have been accustomed to approach God with any mistrust of the kindness of His feelings toward us; if our religious life has been poisoned by fear; if unworthy thoughts of His character and will have filled our hearts with suspicions of His goodness; if we have pictured Him as a self-seeking tyrant; if, in short, we have imagined Him in any way other than that which has been revealed to us in "the face of Jesus Christ"

(2 Corinthians 4:6), we must go back to the records of that lovely life lived among men and must bring our conceptions of God into line with His character and ways.

No one who believes in Christ can doubt that He knew God. He has assured us over and over again that He knew what He was talking about, and that what He said was to be received as the absolute truth, because He had come down from heaven and therefore knew about heavenly things.

None of us would dare to openly question the truth of this, and yet many of God's children ignore Christ's testimony and choose instead to listen to the testimony of their own doubting hearts. If there is one thing taught in the Bible more plainly than any other, it is that the name and the character of His Father that Christ gave must be His real name and character. He declares of Himself over and over that He was a living manifestation of the Father; and in all He said and did He was simply saying and doing what the Father would have said and done had He acted directly out of heaven.

In the face of such unqualified assertions as these out of the lips of our Lord Himself, it becomes not only our privilege but our duty to cast out every element that could in any way conflict with the life and character and teaching of Christ.

As we look at the life of Christ and listen to His words, we can hear God saying, "I am rest for the weary; I am peace for the storm-tossed; I am strength for the strengthless; I am wisdom for the foolish; I am righteousness for the sinful; I am all that the neediest soul on earth can want; I am exceedingly abundantly beyond all you can ask or think."

But here the doubter may say, "No doubt this is all true, but how can I get hold of it? I am so poor and unworthy that I don't dare believe such grace can belong to me."

How can you get hold of it, you ask? You cannot get hold of it at all, but you can let it get hold of you. It is a piece of magnificent good news declared to you in the Bible, and you only need to do with it exactly what you do when any earthly good news is told you by a reliable earthly source. If the speaker is trustworthy, you believe what he says and act in accordance. And you must do the same here. If Christ is trustworthy when He tells you that He is the manifestation of God, you must believe what He says and act accordingly.

You must take your stand on His trustworthiness. You must say to yourself, "I am going to believe what Christ says about God. No matter what my own thoughts and feelings are, nor what anybody else may say, I know that what Christ says about God must be true, for He knew, and I am going to believe Him no matter what. He says that He was one with God, so all that He was God is, and I will never be frightened of God anymore. I will never again let myself think of Him as a stern lawgiver who is angry with me because of my sins, nor as a hard taskmaster who demands from me impossible tasks, nor as a far-off unapproachable deity."

It is unthinkable to suppose that when God told Moses His name was "I am," He could have meant to say, "I am a stern lawgiver," or "I am a hard taskmaster," or "I am a God who is wrapped up in My own glory and am indifferent to the sorrows or fears of My people." If we should try to fill in the blank of His "I am" with such things as these, every Christian in the world would be horrified. But don't the doubts and fears of some of these very Christians say exactly these things in secret every day of their lives?

May God grant that what we learn in our consideration of the names of God make it impossible for us to ever entertain such doubts and fears again.

3
⚗

THE GOD OF ALL COMFORT

Blessed be the God and Father of our Lord Jesus
Christ, the Father of mercies and God of all
comfort, who comforts us in all our tribulation,
that we may be able to comfort those who are in
any trouble, with the comfort with which
we ourselves are comforted by God.

2 CORINTHIANS 1:3–4

Among all the names that reveal God, the God
of all comfort" seems to me one of the love-
liest and most absolutely comforting. The
words "all comfort" speak of no limitation
and no deductions. One would suppose that,
however full of discomforts the outward life

of the followers of such a God might be, their inward life must be a comfortable life. But, as a matter of fact, it often seems as if exactly the opposite were the case: the religious lives of many of the children of God are full of great discomfort. This discomfort arises from anxiety as to their relationship to God and doubts about His love. They torment themselves with the thought that they are too good-for-nothing to be worthy of His care, and they suspect Him of being indifferent to their trials and of forsaking them in times of need. They are anxious and troubled about everything in their religious life, about their feelings, their indifference to the Bible, their lack of fervency in prayer, their coldness of heart. They are tormented with regrets over their past and with devouring anxieties for their future. They feel unworthy to enter God's presence and dare not believe that they belong to Him. They can be happy and comfortable with their earthly friends, but they cannot be happy or comfortable with God. And although He declares Himself to be the God of all comfort, they continually complain that they cannot find comfort anywhere.

Such Christians spread gloom and discomfort wherever they go. I'm afraid that the apparent uncomfortable religious lives of so many Christians is responsible for much of the unbelief of the world.

The apostle Paul says that we are to be living epistles known and read of all men; and the question as to what men read in us is of far more vital importance to the spread of Christ's kingdom than we half the time realize. It is not what we say that tells but what we are. It is easy enough to say many beautiful things about God being the God of all comfort, but unless we know what it is to be really and truly comforted ourselves, we might as well talk to the wind. People must read in our lives what they hear in our words, or all our preaching is worse than useless. We should ask ourselves what they are reading in us. Is it comfort or discomfort that voices itself in our daily walk and life?

But at this point I may be asked what I mean by the comfort God gives. Is it a sort of grace that may prepare us for heaven but is somehow unfit to bear the brunt of our everyday life with its trials and its pains? Or is it an honest and genuine comfort, as we understand comfort, that enfolds life's trials and pains in an all-encompassing peace?

With all my heart I believe it is the latter.

Comfort, whether human or divine, is pure and simple comfort, nothing else. None of us care for pious phrases, we want realities; and the reality of being comforted and comfortable seems to me almost more delightful than any other thing in life. We all know what it is. When as little children we cuddled up in our mother's lap after a fall and felt her loving arms around us, we had comfort. When, as grown-ups, after a hard day's work, we have put on our slippers and seated ourselves by the fire, in an easy chair with a book, we have had comfort. When, after a painful illness, we have begun to recover and have been able to stretch our limbs and open our eyes without pain, we have had comfort. We have probably said a thousand times, with a sigh of relief, when a difficult job is done or a burden is laid down,

"Well, this is comfortable," and in that word *comfortable* there has been comprised more a rest, relief, satisfaction, and pleasure than any other word in the English language could possibly be made to express. We cannot fail, therefore, to understand the meaning of this name of God, the "God of all comfort."

But unfortunately, we have failed to believe it. It has seemed to us too good to be true. The joy and delight of it, if it were really a fact, have been more than our suspicious natures can take in. We may venture to hope sometimes that little scraps of comfort may be granted to us, but we have run away frightened at the thought of the "all comfort" that is ours in the salvation of the Lord Jesus Christ.

And yet what more could He have said about it than He has said: "As one whom his mother comforts, so I will comfort you; and you shall be comforted" (Isaiah 66:13). Notice the *as* and *so* in this passage: "As one whom his mother comforts, so will I comfort you." It is real comforting that is meant here, and yet how many of us have really believed that God's comforting is actually as tender and true as a mother's comforting, or even half or quarter so real. Instead of thinking of ourselves as being hugged to His heart, as a mother's hug, have we not rather been inclined to look upon Him as a stern, unbending judge, holding us at a distance and demanding our respectful homage, critical of our slightest faults? Is it any wonder that our religion has made us thoroughly uncomfortable? Who could help being uncomfortable in the presence of such a judge?

But I am happy to say that that stern judge is not there. He does not exist. The God who does exist is a God who is like a mother. Over and over again He declares this. "I, even I, am He who comforts you" (Isaiah 51:12), He says to the frightened children of Israel. And then He reproaches them for not being comforted. "Why," He says, "should you let anything make you afraid when here is the Lord, your Maker, ready and longing to comfort you? You have feared the fury of the oppressor and have forgotten Me. Where is the fury of the oppressor when I am nearby?"

The God who exists is the God and the Father of our Lord Jesus Christ, the God who so loved the world that He sent His Son, not to judge the world, but to save it. He is the God who anointed the Lord Jesus Christ to bind up the brokenhearted, to proclaim liberty to the captives and the opening of the prison to those who are bound, and to comfort all who mourn. Please notice that *all*. Not a few select people, but all. Every captive of sin, every prisoner in infirmity, every mourning heart throughout the whole world must be included in this "all." It would not be "all" if there should be a single one left out, no matter how insignificant or unworthy or even how fainthearted that one might be. I have always been thankful that the fainthearted are especially mentioned by Paul in his exhortations to the Thessalonian Christians, when he is urging them to comfort one another. In effect he says, Do not scold the fainthearted but comfort them (see 1 Thessalonians 5:14). The very ones who need comfort most are the ones that our God wants to comfort—not the strong-minded ones but the fainthearted.

The Lord Jesus Christ was anointed to comfort "all who mourn." The "God of all comfort" sent His Son to be the comforter of a mourning world. And all through His life on earth He fulfilled His divine mission. When His disciples asked Him to call down fire from heaven to consume some people who refused to receive Him, He rebuked them and said: "You do not know what manner of spirit you are of. For the Son of Man did not come to destroy men's lives but to save them" (Luke 9:55–56). He received sinners and ate with them. He welcomed Mary Magdalene when all men turned from her. He refused even to condemn the woman who was taken in the very act of sin. Always and everywhere He was on the side of sinners. That was what He was for. He came to save sinners. He had no other mission.

If any troubled heart that is constantly fearful should read these lines, let me tell you again that this is just what the Lord Jesus Christ is for—to care for and comfort all who mourn. "All," remember, every single one, even you yourself, for it would not be "all" if you were left out. You may be so discouraged that you can hardly lift up your head, but the apostle tells us that He is the "God who comforts the downcast" (2 Corinthians 7:6).

And our Comforter is not far off in heaven where we cannot find Him. He is close at hand. He abides with us. When Christ was going away from this earth, He told His disciples that He would not leave them comfortless but would send "another Comforter" who would abide with them forever. This Comforter, He said, would teach them all things and would remind them of all things. And then He declared: "Peace I leave with you, My peace I give to you; not as the world gives do I give to you. Let not your heart be troubled, neither let it be afraid" (John 14:27).

Comforter—what a word of bliss. And an "abiding" Comforter, too, not one who comes and goes and is never on hand when most needed, but one who is always present and always ready to give us "joy for mourning, the garment of praise for the spirit of heaviness" (Isaiah 61:3).

The very words "abiding Comforter" are an amazing revelation. If we can have a human comforter to stay with us for only a few days when we are in trouble, we think ourselves fortunate; but here is a divine Comforter who is always staying with us and whose power to comfort is infinite. We should never be without comfort or ever be uncomfortable.

But you may ask whether this divine Comforter does not sometimes reprove us for our sins and whether we can get any comfort out of this. In my opinion, this is exactly one of the places where the comfort comes in. For what sort of people would we be if we had no divine Teacher always at hand to show us our faults and awaken in us a desire to get rid of them?

If I am walking along the street with an ugly hole in the back of my dress, of which I am ignorant, it would be a comfort to me if a kind friend pointed it out to me. Similarly, it is a comfort to know that there is always abiding with me a divine, all-seeing Comforter who will reprove me for all my faults and will not let me go on in a fatal unconsciousness of them.

You may object, perhaps, because you are not worthy of His comforts. I do not suppose you are. No one ever is. But you need His comforting, and because you are not worthy you need it all the more. Christ came into the world to save sinners, not good people, and your unworthiness is your greatest claim to His salvation.

In the same passage in Isaiah in which He tells us that He has seen our ways and was angry with us, He assures us that He will heal us and restore comforts to us (see Isaiah 57:18). It is just because He is angry with us (angry in the sense in which love is always angry with any fault in those it loves) that He "restores comforts" to us. And He does it by revealing our sin and healing it.

The avenue to the comforting of the divine Comforter lies through the need of comfort. And this explains to me better than anything else the reason why the Lord so often allows sorrow and trial to be our portion. "Therefore, behold, I will allure her, will bring her into the wilderness, and speak comfort to her" (Hosea 2:14). We may find ourselves in a "wilderness" of disappointment and suffering, and we wonder why the God who loves us should have allowed it. But He knows that it is only in that very wilderness that we can hear and receive the "comfortable words" He has to pour out on us. We must feel the need for comfort before we can listen to the words of comfort. And God knows that it is infinitely better for us to need His comforts and receive them than it could ever be to not need them and so be without them. The consolations of God mean the substituting of a far higher and better thing for what we lose to get them. The things we lose are earthly things, those He substitutes are heavenly. And who of us would thankfully be "allured" by our God into any earthly wilderness if only there we might find the unspeakable joys of union with Himself. Paul could say he "counted all things but loss" if he might but "win Christ," and if we have even the faintest glimpse of what winning Christ means, we will say so too.

Strangely enough, it is easy for us when we are happy and don't need comforting to believe that our God is the "God of all comfort," but as soon as we are in trouble and need it, it seems impossible to believe that there can be any comfort for us anywhere. It would almost seem as if, in our reading of the Bible, we had reversed its meaning and made it say, not "Blessed are they that mourn, for they shall be comforted," but "Blessed are they that rejoice, for they, and they only, shall be comforted." In our secret hearts we almost unconsciously alter the Bible words a little and make the meaning exactly opposite to what it actually is; or else we put in so many "ifs" and "buts" as to take the whole point out of what is said. Let's take, for instance, the beautiful words "God, who comforts the downcast" (2 Corinthians 7:6) and ask ourselves whether we have ever been tempted to make it read in our secret hearts, "God, who forsakes the downcast," or, "God, who overlooks the downcast," or, "God, who will comfort those who are downcast if they show themselves worthy of comfort." And instead of being comforted, we have been plunged into misery and despair.

The psalmist tells us that God will "comfort us on every side" (see Psalm 71:21), and what an all-embracing comfort this is. "On everyside," no aching spot left uncomforted. And yet, in times of special trial, how many Christians secretly read this as though it said, "God will comfort us on every side except just the side where our trials lie; on that side there is no comfort anywhere"? But God says every side.

Sadly, too many of us are like Israel of old. When God said to Zion: "Sing, O heavens! Be joyful, O earth! And break out in singing, O mountains! For the LORD has comforted His people, and will have mercy on His afflicted" (Isaiah 49:13), Zion replied, "The LORD has forsaken me, and my Lord has forgotten me" (Isaiah 49:14). And then God's answer came in these wonderful words: "Can a woman forget her nursing child, and not have compassion on the son of her womb? Surely they may forget, yet I will not forget you. See, I have inscribed you on the palms of My hands; your walls are continually before Me" (Isaiah 49:15–16).

But how do you get hold of this divine comfort, you may ask. My answer is that you must take it. God's comfort is being continually and abundantly given, but unless you accept it you can't have it.

Divine comfort does not come to us in any mysterious or arbitrary way. It comes as the result of a divine method. The indwelling Comforter "brings to our remembrance" comforting things concerning our Lord, and if we believe them, we are comforted by them. A verse is brought to our remembrance maybe, or the verse of a song, or some thought about the love of Christ and His tender care for us. If we receive the suggestion in simple faith, we can't help being comforted. But if we refuse to listen to the voice of our Comforter and listen instead to the voice of discouragement or despair, no comfort can reach our souls.

The apostle Paul tells us that everything written in the Scriptures is for our learning, in order that we "through the patience and comfort of the Scriptures might have hope" (Romans 15:4). Nothing God has said can possibly comfort a person who doesn't believe it to be true. Comfort must follow faith and can never precede it.

In this matter of comfort it is exactly as it is in every other experience in the religious life. God says, "Believe, and then you can feel." We say, "Feel, and then we can believe." God's order is not arbitrary, it exists in the very nature of things. I couldn't feel glad that I had a fortune in the bank unless I knew that it was really there. But in spiritual things we reverse God's order and refuse to believe that we possess anything until we first feel we have it.

Let me illustrate. Let's say we are overwhelmed with cares and anxieties. To comfort us in these circumstances the Lord assures us that we don't need to be anxious about anything but may commit all our cares to Him, for He cares for us. We are all familiar with the passages where He tells us to "look at the birds of the air" (Matthew 6:26) and to "consider the lilies of the field" (Matthew 6:28). He assures us that we are of much more value than they, and that, if He cares for them, He will much more care for us. One would think there was comfort enough here for every care or sorrow in the whole world. To have almighty God—who can control and foresee everything and manage everything in the best possible way—carry our cares and burdens for us, what could possibly be a greater comfort? Then why are so few people comforted by this truth? Simply because they don't believe it. They are waiting to have an inward feeling that His words are true before they will believe them.

The remedy is plain. If we want to be comforted, we must make up our minds to believe every single solitary word of comfort God has ever spoken. We must resolutely determine to believe in the divine Comforter and to accept and rejoice in His all-embracing comfort. We must put our wills into this matter of being comforted. We must choose to be comforted.

Whoever adopts this plan will come, sooner or later, into a state of abounding comfort.

4
❧

THE LORD OUR SHEPHERD

The LORD is my shepherd;
I shall not want.
PSALM 23:1

Perhaps no aspect of the Lord's character is more full of genuine comfort than the aspect expressed in the twenty-third Psalm, and in its corresponding passage in the tenth chapter of John.

The psalmist tells me that the Lord is my Shepherd, and the Lord Himself declares that He is the good Shepherd. Can anything be more comforting?

How many of us remember learning the

twenty-third Psalm as children and the joy and pride of our childish hearts when we were first able to repeat it without any mistakes? Since then we have always known it, but at this moment maybe its words sound so old and familiar to some of you that you cannot see what meaning they can convey.

But in truth they tell us the whole story of our religion in words of such wonderful depth of meaning that I doubt anyone has ever been able to fully grasp the things they reveal.

Repeat these familiar words to yourselves: "The Lord is my shepherd, I shall not want."

Who is it that is your shepherd?

The Lord! What a wonderful announcement! The Lord God of heaven and earth, the almighty Creator of all things, who holds the universe in His hand, He is your Shepherd and has charged Himself with the care and keeping of you as a shepherd is charged with the care and keeping of his sheep.

If your hearts will only take in this thought, I can promise you that your religion will from now on be full of the deepest comfort, and your old uncomfortable religion will drop off forever.

I had a vivid experience of this at one time in my Christian life. The twenty-third Psalm had, of course, always been familiar to me, but it had never seemed to have any special meaning. Then came a critical moment in my life when I was in need of comfort but couldn't find it anywhere. I could not at the moment lay my hands on my Bible, and I searched in my mind for some passage of Scripture that would help me. Immediately these flashed into my mind: "The Lord is my shepherd, I shall not want." At first I turned from them almost with scorn, and I tried hard to think of a more profound one but nothing would come. Finally it almost seemed as if there were no other verses in the whole Bible, and I was reduced to saying, "Well, if I can't think of any other verse, I should at least try to get what little good I can out of this one." I began to repeat to myself over and over, "The Lord is my shepherd, I shall not want." Suddenly, as I did so, the words were divinely illuminated, and there poured out on me such floods of comfort that I felt I could never have a trouble again.

The moment I could get hold of a Bible I turned its pages with eagerness to see whether it could possibly be true that such untold treasures of comfort were actually mine and whether I might dare to fully enjoy them. And I did what I have often found great benefit in doing: I built up a pyramid of declarations and promises concerning the Lord being our Shepherd that, once built, presented an immovable and indestructible front to all the winds and storms of doubt or trial that could assail it. I became convinced, beyond a shadow of a doubt, that the Lord really was my Shepherd, and that in giving Himself this name He assumed the duties belonging to the name.

He Himself draws the contrast between a good shepherd and a bad shepherd when He follows up His announcement "I am the good shepherd" (John 10:11) with the words, "But a hireling, he who is not the shepherd, one who does not own the sheep, sees the wolf coming and leaves the sheep and flees;

and the wolf catches the sheep and scatters them" (John 10:12). Through the prophets the Lord pours down condemnation upon all such faithless shepherds. "And the LORD said to me," said the prophet Zechariah, "take for yourself the implements of a foolish shepherd. . . . Woe to the worthless shepherd, who leaves the flock! A sword shall be against his arm and against his right eye; his arm shall completely wither, and his right eye shall be totally blinded" (Zechariah 11:15, 17).

Again the prophet Ezekiel says: "Thus says the Lord GOD to the shepherds: 'Woe to the shepherds of Israel who feed themselves! Should not the shepherds feed the flocks? . . .The weak you have not strengthened, nor have you healed those who were sick, nor bound up the broken, nor brought back what was driven away, nor sought what was lost; but with force and cruelty you have ruled them. . . .' Therefore, O shepherds, hear the word of the LORD! Thus says the Lord GOD: 'Behold, I am against the shepherds, and I will require My flock at their hand; I will cause them to cease feeding the sheep, and the shepherds shall feed themselves no more; for I will deliver My flock from their mouths'" (Ezekiel 34:2, 4, 9–10).

It's hard to believe that any Christian could ever accuse our divine Shepherd of being as faithless and unkind as those He condemned through the prophets. And yet if some Christian hearts could be revealed, it would be found that such are their feelings about Him. What else can it mean when Christians complain that the Lord has forsaken them; that they cry to Him for spiritual food and He doesn't hear; that they are surrounded by enemies and He doesn't deliver them; that when their souls find themselves in dark places He doesn't come to their rescue; that when they are weak He doesn't strengthen them; and when they are spiritually sick He doesn't heal them?

What are all these doubts and discouragements but secret accusations against our good Shepherd of the very things He Himself so scathingly condemns?

You have said, I know, hundreds of times, "The Lord is my shepherd," but have you ever really believed it to be a fact? Have you felt safe and happy and free from care, as a sheep must feel when under the care of a good shepherd, or have you felt like a poor forlorn sheep without a shepherd, or a sheep with an unfaithful, inefficient shepherd who doesn't supply your needs and leaves you in times of danger and darkness?

Have you had a comfortable religious life or an uncomfortable one? If the latter has been your condition, how can you reconcile it with the statement that the Lord is your Shepherd, and therefore you shall not want? You say He is your Shepherd, and yet you complain that you do want. Who has made the mistake? You or the Lord?

But here, perhaps, you will meet me with the words, "Oh, no, I don't blame the Lord, but I am so weak and foolish and ignorant that I am not worthy of His care." But don't you know that sheep are always weak and helpless and silly, and that the very reason a shepherd cares for them is because they are so unable to take care of themselves? Their welfare and their safety do not in the least depend upon their own strength or their wisdom or on anything in themselves, but completely on the care of their shepherd. And if you are a sheep, you also must depend completely on your Shepherd.

Let's imagine two flocks of sheep meeting at the end of the winter to compare their experiences—one flock fat and strong and in good condition, and the other poor and lean and diseased. Will the healthy flock boast and say, "See what fabulous care we have taken of ourselves, what good, strong, wise sheep we must be"? Of course not. Their boasting would all be about their shepherd. "See what a good shepherd we have had," they would say, "and how he has cared for us. Through all the storms of the winter he has protected us and defended us from every wild beast and has always provided us with the best of food."

On the other hand, would the poor diseased sheep blame themselves and say, "What wicked sheep we must be to be in such poor shape!" No, they too would speak only of their shepherd, but how different would be their story! "Sadly," they would say, "our shepherd was very different from yours! He fed himself, but he did not feed us. He did not strengthen us when we were weak, nor heal us when we were sick, nor bandage us up when we were broken nor look for us when we were lost. Oh, that we had had a good shepherd like yours!"

We all understand this responsibility of the shepherd in the case of sheep, but the moment we transfer the figure to our religion, we at once shift all the responsibility off the Shepherd's shoulders and lay it on the sheep, and demand of the poor human sheep the wisdom, care, and power to provide that can only belong to the divine Shepherd. Of course the poor human sheep fail and their religious lives become thoroughly uncomfortable.

I freely confess there is a difference between sheep and ourselves in this, that they have neither the intelligence nor the power to withdraw themselves from the care of their shepherd, while we have. We are so much wiser than sheep, in our own estimation, that we think the sort of trust sheep exercise won't do for us. In our superior intelligence, we presume to take matters into our own hands and so cut ourselves off from the Shepherd's care.

Now, if any sheep in the flock of Christ find themselves in a poor condition, there are only two explanations possible. Either the Lord is not a good Shepherd and doesn't care for His sheep, or else His sheep have not believed in His care and have been afraid or ashamed to trust themselves to it. I know not one of you will dare to say, or even think, that the Lord can be anything but a good Shepherd. The fault, therefore, must lie here: either you have not believed He was your Shepherd at all, or else, believing it, you have refused to let Him take care of you.

I strongly encourage you to face this matter boldly and give yourself a definite answer. For not only are your own welfare and comfort dependent upon your right understanding of this beautiful relationship, but also the glory of your Shepherd is at stake. Have you ever thought of the grief and dishonor this sad condition of yours brings on Him? The credit of a shepherd depends on the condition of his flock. He might boast about his qualifications as a shepherd, but it would be all for nothing if the flocks he had charge of were in a diseased condition, with many missing and many with lean ribs and broken bones.

If an owner of sheep is thinking of employing a shepherd, he requires a reference from the shepherd's last employer, that he might learn from him how his flock fared under this shepherd's care. Now, the Lord makes statements about Himself as a good Shepherd. He is telling the universe, the world, and the Church, "I am the good shepherd." And if they ask, "Where are Your sheep, what condition are they in?" can He point to us as being a credit to His care? And is it not grievous if any of us refuse to let the Shepherd take care of us, and so bring discredit to His name by our sad condition? The universe is watching to see what the Lord Jesus Christ is able to make of us, and what kind of sheep we are, whether we are well fed, healthy, and happy. Their verdict concerning Him will largely depend upon what they see in us.

When Paul was writing to the Ephesians that he had been called to preach to the Gentiles the unsearchable riches of Christ and make all men see the fellowship of the mystery that had been hidden in God from the beginning of the world, he added the significant words that the purpose of it all was "to the intent that now the manifold wisdom of God might be made known by the church to the principalities and powers in the heavenly places, according to the eternal purpose which He accomplished in Christ Jesus our Lord" (Ephesians 3:10–11).

Well may we be lost in amazement at the thought that God has purposed such a glorious destiny for His sheep as to make known to the universe His "manifold wisdom" by what He has done for us! Surely this should make us eager to abandon ourselves to Him in the most generous trust for salvation, that He may get great glory in the universe and the whole world may be won to trust Him.

But if we will not let Him save us, if we reject His care and refuse to feed in His pastures or lie down in His fold, then we shall be a starved and shivering flock, sick and full of complaints, bringing dishonor on Him and hindering the world from coming to Him.

No wonder unbelievers aren't drawn into the church. No wonder that in some churches there are no conversions from one end of the year to the other. We must have a fold that shows sheep in good condition if we expect outsiders to come in.

You can't fail to care about the dishonor you bring upon your divine Shepherd by your poor condition. You long to serve Him and bring Him glory, and you can do it if you will only show to the whole world that He is a Shepherd whom it is safe to trust.

Let me help you do this. First face the fact of what a Shepherd must be and do in order to be a good Shepherd, and then face the fact that the Lord is really a good Shepherd. Then say the words over to yourself with all the willpower you can muster, "The Lord is my Shepherd. He is. No matter what I feel, He says He is, and He is. I am going to believe it, come what may." Then repeat the words with a different emphasis each time:

The *Lord* is my Shepherd.

The Lord *is* my Shepherd.

The Lord is *my* Shepherd.

The Lord is my *Shepherd*.

Visualize what your ideal Shepherd would be, and then know that an ideal far beyond yours was in the mind of our Lord when He said, "I am the good shepherd." He knew the sheep He had undertaken to save, and He knew that the Shepherd is responsible for His flock and that He is bound to care for them and to bring them all home safely to the Master's fold. Therefore, He said: "This is the will of the Father who sent Me, that of all he has given Me I should lose nothing, but should raise it up at the last day" (John 6:39). Again He said, "The good shepherd gives His life for the sheep" (John 10:11). And still again: "My sheep hear My voice, and I know them, and they follow Me. And I give them eternal life, and they shall never perish; neither shall anyone snatch them out of My hand" (John 10:27–28).

Centuries before Jesus came to be the Shepherd, the Father said: "Therefore I will save my flock, and they shall no longer be a prey; and I will judge between sheep and sheep. I will establish one shepherd over them, and he shall feed them—My servant David. He shall feed them and be their shepherd" (Ezekiel 34:22–23). I catch a glimpse of the Father's yearning love in these words. He has undertaken His duties, knowing perfectly well what the responsibilities are. He knows that He has to do with silly sheep, who have no strength to protect themselves, no wisdom to guide themselves, and nothing to recommend them but their utter helplessness and weakness. But none of these things baffle Him. His strength and His skill are sufficient to meet every emergency that can possibly arise.

There is only one thing that can hinder Him, and that is if the sheep will not trust Him and refuse to let Him take care of them.

Lose sight of yourself for a moment and try to put yourself in the Shepherd's place.

Consider your condition as He considers it. See Him coming out to seek you in your far-off wandering. See His tender, yearning love, His longing to save you. Believe His own description of Himself, and take Him at His own sweet word.

Begin to trust and follow your Shepherd now and here. Abandon yourself to His care and guidance and trust Him utterly.

You don't need to be afraid to follow Him wherever He leads, for He always leads His sheep into green pastures and beside still waters. Even though you may seem to yourself to be in the midst of a desert, with nothing green around you inwardly or outwardly, the good Shepherd will turn the place where you are into green pastures. He has promised that "instead of the thorn shall come up the cypress tree, and instead of the brier shall come up the myrtle tree" (Isaiah 55:13); and "waters shall burst forth in the wilderness, and streams in the desert" (Isaiah 35:6).

Or perhaps you may say, "My life is a tempest of sorrow or temptation, and it will be a long time before I can walk beside any still waters." But hasn't your Shepherd said to the raging seas before this, "Peace, be still! . . . And there was a great calm" (Mark 4:39)? And can't He do it again?

Thousands can testify that when they have put themselves absolutely into His hands, He has quieted the raging tempest and has turned their deserts into blossoming gardens. I don't mean that there will be no more outward trouble or care or suffering, but these very places will become green pastures and still waters inwardly to the soul. The Shepherd knows what pastures are best for His sheep. Perhaps He sees that the best pastures for some of us are to be found in the midst of opposition or earthly trials. If He leads you there, you may be sure they are green pastures for you and that you will grow to be made strong by feeding in them.

But words fail to tell the half of what the good Shepherd does for the flock that trusts Him. He does indeed, according to His promise, make with them a covenant of peace and causes the evil beasts to die out of the land. They will dwell safely in the wilderness and sleep in the woods. He makes them and the places around them a blessing; and He causes the rain to come down in its season, and there are showers of blessing. The tree of the field yields its fruit, and the earth yields her increase. They are safe in their land and are no longer a prey to the heathen, and no one can make them afraid.

Now you will probably ask me how you can get the Lord to be your Shepherd. My answer is that you don't need to get Him to be your Shepherd, because He already is your Shepherd. All that is needed is for you to recognize that He is, and yield yourself to His control.

When the announcement is made in a family to the children who have been longing for a little sister that one has just been born to them, they don't go on saying, "Oh, how we wish we had a little sister!" or, "What can we do to get a little sister?" But they begin at once to shout for joy and dance about calling out to everybody, "Hurray! Hurray! We have a little sister now."

And since the announcement has been made to all of us that He is our Savior, we must begin at once to rejoice that He is and give ourselves into His care. Every soul that will begin from today to believe in the good Shepherd and trust His care will sooner or later find itself feeding in His green pastures and walking beside His still waters.

What else can the Lord do with His sheep but this? He has no folds that are not good folds, no pastures that are not green pastures, and no waters but still waters. They may not look so outwardly, but we who have tried them can testify that His fold and His pastures are always places of peace and comfort to the inward life of the soul.

If you have difficulty understanding all this, I would advise you not to try to understand it but simply to begin to live it. Just take the psalm and say, "This is my psalm, and I am going to believe it. I have always known it by heart, but it has never meant much to me. But now I have made up my mind to believe that the Lord really is my Shepherd and that He will care for me as a shepherd cares for his sheep. I will not doubt or question it again." And then just abandon yourself to His care, trusting Him fully and following wherever He leads.

With the Lord for our Shepherd, how is it possible for anything to go wrong? With Him for our Shepherd, all that this psalm promises must be ours. And when we have learned to know Him in this way, we will be able to say with triumphant trust: "Surely goodness and mercy shall follow me [pursue, overtake] all the days of my life; and I will dwell in the house of the LORD forever" (Psalm 23:6). Even the future will lose all its terror, and our confidence in our Shepherd will deliver us from all fear of bad news.

If each one of you will enter into this relationship with Christ and really be a helpless, trusting sheep, believing Him to be your Shepherd, and will follow Him wherever He leads, you will soon lose all your old spiritual discomfort and know the peace of God that surpasses all understanding to keep your hearts and minds in Christ Jesus (see Philippians 4:7).

5

❦

HE SPOKE TO THEM
OF THE FATHER

They did not understand that
He spoke to them of the Father.
JOHN 8:27

One of the most illuminating names of God is the one especially revealed by our Lord Jesus Christ, the name of Father. I say especially revealed by Christ, because, while God had been called throughout the ages by many other names, Christ alone has revealed Him to us under the all-inclusive name of Father—a name that holds within itself all other names of wisdom and power, of love and goodness, a name that embodies for us a perfect supply for all our needs.

In the Old Testament God was not revealed as the Father so much as a great warrior fighting for His people, or as a mighty king ruling over them and caring for them. The name of Father is only given to Him a few times there, six or seven times at the most, while in the New Testament it is given about two or three hundred times. Christ, who knew Him, was the only one who could reveal Him. "No one," He said, "knows who the Father is except the Son, and the one to whom the Son wills to reveal Him" (Luke 10:22).

The vital question then that confronts each one of us is whether we understand that Christ speaks to us of the Father. We know He uses the word *Father* continually, but do we understand what the word really means? Have we even an inkling of what the Father is?

So many of God's children think of Him as a stern judge or a severe taskmaster, or at the best as an unapproachable dignitary, seated on a far-off throne, dispensing exacting laws for a frightened and trembling world. But they have no concept of a God who is a Father, tender, loving, and full of compassion, who will be on their side against the whole universe.

It is a Father such as our highest instincts tell us a good father ought to be of whom I am speaking. Sometimes earthly fathers are unkind, tyrannical, selfish, or even cruel, or they are merely indifferent and neglectful; but none of these can be called good fathers. But God, who is good, must be a good father or not a father at all. We must all of us have known good fathers in this world, or at least can imagine them.

But God is not only a father, He is a mother as well, and we have all of us known mothers whose love and tenderness have been without bound or limit. And it is very certain that the God who created them both, and who is Himself father and mother in one, could never have created earthly fathers and mothers who were more tender and more loving than He is Himself. Therefore if we want to know what sort of a Father He is, we must heap together all the best of all the fathers and mothers we have ever known or can imagine, and we must tell ourselves that this is only a faint image of our Father in heaven.

When our Lord was teaching His disciples how to pray, the only name by which He taught them to address God was "Our Father in heaven." And this surely meant that we were to think of Him only in this light. Millions of times during all the centuries since then has this name been uttered by the children of God everywhere, and yet how much has it been understood? Had all who used the name known what it meant, it would have been impossible for the misrepresentations of His character and the doubts of His love and care that have so desolated the souls of His children throughout all the ages to have crept in. Moreover, since He is an "everlasting Father," He must act, always and under all circumstances, as a good father ought to act. It is inconceivable that a good father could forget or neglect or be unfair to his children. A savage father might, or a wicked father, but a good father never! And in calling our God by the blessed name of Father, we ought to know that, if He is a father at all, He must be the very best of fathers, and His fatherhood must be the highest ideal of fatherhood of which we can conceive.

But, you may say, what about the other names of God, do they not convey other and more terrifying ideas? They only do so because this blessed name of Father is not added to them. This name must underlie every other name by which He has ever been known. Has He been called a judge? Yes, but He is a father judge, one who judges as a loving father would. Is He a king? Yes, but He is a king who is at the same time the Father of His subjects, and who rules them with a father's tenderness. Is He a lawgiver? Yes, but He is a lawgiver who gives laws as a father would, remembering the weakness and ignorance of His helpless children. "As a father pities his children, so the LORD pities those who fear Him. For He knows our frame; He remembers that we are dust" (Psalm 103:13–14). It is not "as a judge judges, so the Lord judges"; not "as a taskmaster controls, so the Lord controls"; not "as a lawgiver imposes laws, so the Lord imposes laws"; but, "as a father pities, so the Lord pities."

Never must we think of God in any other way than as our Father. What a good father could not do, God cannot do either; and what a good father ought to do, God is absolutely sure to do.

In our Lord's last prayer in John 17, He says that He has declared to us the name of the Father in order that we may discover the wonderful fact that the Father loves us as He loved His Son, yet do any of us believe that it is an actual, tangible fact that God loves us as much as He loved Christ? If we believed this to be actually the case, could we ever have an anxious or rebellious thought again? Would we not be absolutely and utterly sure under every conceivable circumstance that the divine Father would care for us in the best possible way?

It is very striking that He so often said, "Your heavenly Father, not Mine only, but yours just as much. Your heavenly Father,"

He says, "cares for the sparrows and the lilies, and of course He will care for you who are of so much more value than many sparrows." How supremely foolish it is then for us to be worried and anxious about things, when Christ has said that our heavenly Father knows that we have need of all these things!

What can be the matter with us that we don't understand this?

Again, our Lord draws the comparison between earthly fathers and our heavenly Father in order to show us, not how much less good and tender and willing to bless is our heavenly Father but how much more. " 'If you then, being evil,'" He says, "'know how to give good gifts to your children, how much more will your Father who is in heaven give good things to those who ask Him!' " (Matthew 7:11). Can we imagine a good earthly father giving a stone or a snake to a hungry child instead of bread or fish? Would not our whole souls be repulsed by a father who could do such things? And yet I fear many of God's children actually think that their heavenly Father does this sort of thing to them.

But it is not only that our heavenly Father is willing to give us good things. He is far more than willing. Our Lord says, "Do not fear, little flock, for it is your Father's good pleasure to give you the kingdom" (Luke 12:32). There is no grudging in His giving, it is His "good pleasure" to give; He likes to do it. He wants to give you the kingdom far more than you want to have it. Those of us who are parents know how eager we are to give good things to our children, and this may help us understand how it is God's "good pleasure" to give us the kingdom. Why, then, should we ask Him with such fear, and why should we be anxious that He might fail to grant what we need?

There can be only one answer to these questions: we don't know the Father.

We are told that we are of the "household of God." Now the principle is announced in the Bible that if any man provides not for his own household, he has "denied the faith and is worse than an unbeliever" (1 Timothy 5:8). Since then we are of the "household of God," this principle applies to Him, and if He should fail to provide for us, His own words would condemn Him. I say this reverently, but I want to say it emphatically, for so few people seem to understand it.

If God is our Father, the only thing we can do with doubts and fears and anxious thoughts is to cast them behind our backs forever. If once we see that our doubts are an actual sin against God and imply a question of His trustworthiness, we will be eager to do it. We may have cherished our doubts to this point because we thought they were a part of our religion and an attractive attitude of soul in one so unworthy; but if we now see that God is truly our Father, we will reject every doubt with horror as being a libel on our Father's love and care.

"Behold," says the apostle John, "what manner of love the Father has bestowed on us, that we should be called children of God!" (1 John 3:1). The "manner of love" bestowed on us is the love of a father for his son, a tender, protecting love that knows our weakness and our need and cares for us accordingly. He treats us as sons, and all He asks in return is that we treat Him as a Father we can trust without anxiety. We must take the son's place of dependence and trust and let Him keep the father's place of care and responsibility. Too often we take upon our own shoulders the father's part and try to take care of and provide for ourselves. But no good earthly father would want his children to take on their young shoulders the burden of his duties; much less would our heavenly Father want to lay on us the burden of His.

No wonder we are told to cast all our care on Him, for He cares for us. He would not be a good Father if He didn't. All He asks of us is that we let Him know when we need anything and then leave the supplying of that need to Him. He assures us that if we do this, the "peace of God, which surpasses all understanding, will guard your hearts and minds" (Philippians 4:7). The children of a good, human father are at peace because they trust in their father's care; but the children of the heavenly Father too often have no peace because they are afraid to trust in His care. They make their requests known to Him perhaps, but that is all they do. It is a sort of religious form they feel it necessary to go through. But as to supposing that He really will care for them, no such idea seems to cross their minds, and they go on carrying their cares and burdens on their own shoulders.

What utter folly it all is! For if ever an earthly father was worthy of the confidence of his children, surely much more is our heavenly Father worthy of our confidence.

The remedy for our discomfort and unrest is in becoming acquainted with the Father.

"For," says the apostle Paul, "you did not receive the spirit of bondage again to fear, but you received the spirit of adoption by whom we cry out, 'Abba, Father'" (Romans 8:15). Is it this "Spirit of adoption" that reigns in your heart, or is it the "spirit of bondage"? Your whole comfort in the religious life depends upon which spirit it is.

But you may ask how you are to get this "spirit of adoption." I can only say that it is not a thing to be gotten. It comes, and it comes as the necessary result of the discovery that God is truly a real Father. When we have made this discovery, we cannot help feeling and acting like a child, and this is what the "spirit of adoption" means. It is nothing mystical nor mysterious; it is the simple natural result of having found a Father where you thought there was only a judge.

The great need for every soul, therefore, is to make this supreme discovery. And to do this we have only to see what Christ tells us about the Father, and then believe it.

"If you had known Me," says Christ, "you would have known My Father also; and from now on you know Him and have seen Him" (John 14:7). The thing for us to do then is to make up our minds that from now on we will receive His testimony and will "know the Father."

6
ଔ

JEHOVAH

That they may know that You,
whose name alone is the LORD,
are the Most High over all the earth.
PSALM 83:18

Of all the names of God perhaps the most comprehensive is the name Jehovah. The word *Jehovah* means "the self-existing One, the I am," and it is generally used as a direct revelation of what God is. In several places an explanatory word is added, revealing one of His special characteristics, and it is to these that I want to particularly call attention. They are as follows:

- Jehovah-jireh: the Lord will see,
  or the Lord will provide
- Jehovah-nissi: the Lord
  my Banner
- Jehovah-shalom: the Lord
  our Peace
- Jehovah-tsidkenu: the Lord
  our Righteousness
- Jehovah-shammah: the Lord
  is there

These names were discovered by God's people in times of sore need; that is, the characteristics they describe were discovered, and the names were the natural expression of these characteristics.

When Abraham was about to sacrifice his son and saw no way out, the Lord provided a lamb for the sacrifice and delivered Isaac. Abraham made the grand discovery that it was one of the characteristics of Jehovah to see and provide for the needs of His people. Therefore he called Him Jehovah-jireh—the Lord will see, or the Lord will provide.

The counterparts to this in the New

Testament are numerous. Over and over our Lord urges us to take no care, because God cares for us. "Your heavenly Father knows," He says, "that you need all these things" (Matthew 6:32). If the Lord sees and knows our needs, of course He will provide for them. Being our Father, He can't do anything else. As soon as a good mother sees that her child needs anything, she sets about supplying that need. She doesn't even wait for the child to ask, the sight of the need is asking enough.

When God, therefore, says to us, "I am He who sees your need," He in reality says also, "I am He who provides," for He cannot see and fail to provide.

"Why do I not have everything I want, then?" you may ask. Only because God sees that what you want is not really the thing you need, but probably exactly the opposite. Often, in order to give us what we need, the Lord is obliged to keep from us what we want. Your heavenly Father knows what you need; you don't know. And if all your wants were gratified, it might well be that all your needs would be left unsupplied. It ought to be enough for us that our God is indeed Jehovah-jireh, the Lord who will see, and who will therefore provide.

But many Christians today have never made Abraham's discovery and don't know that the Lord is really Jehovah-jireh. They are trusting Him, it may be, to save their souls in the future, but they never dream He wants to carry their cares for them now and here. They are like a man I heard of who had a heavy load on his back and was offered a lift by a friend. He climbed up into the carriage with gratitude but kept his burden on his back, sitting there bowed down under the weight of it. "Why don't you put your burden down on the bottom of the carriage?" asked his friend.

"Oh," replied the man, "it's a big enough deal to ask you to carry me myself, and I couldn't ask you to carry my burden also." You wonder that anyone could be so foolish, and yet are you not doing the same? Are you not trusting the Lord to take care of yourself but are still carrying your burdens on your own shoulders?

Jehovah-nissi, "the Lord my banner," was

a discovery made by Moses when Amalek came to fight with Israel in Rephidim and the Lord gave the Israelites a glorious victory. Moses realized that the Lord was fighting for them, and he built an altar to Jehovah-nissi, "the Lord my banner." The Bible is full of developments of this name. "The LORD is a man of war" (Exodus 15:3); "The LORD your God is he who fights for you" (Joshua 23:10); "The LORD will fight for you, and you shall hold your peace" (Exodus 14:14); "Do not be afraid nor dismayed because of this great multitude, for the battle is not yours, but God's" (2 Chronicles 20:15); "God Himself is with us as our head" (2 Chronicles 13:12).

The Lord will fight for us if we will just let Him. He knows that we have no strength or power against our spiritual enemies, and like a tender mother when her helpless children are attacked by an enemy, He fights for us. All He asks of us is to be still and let Him. This is the only sort of spiritual conflict that is ever successful. But we are very slow to learn this, and when temptations come, instead of handing the battle over to the

Lord, we summon all our forces to fight them ourselves. We believe, perhaps, that the Lord is somewhere near and, if worst comes to worst, will step in to help us, but mostly we feel that we ourselves must do all the fighting. Our method of fighting generally consists of repenting and making resolutions and promises, wearily struggling for victory, and then failing again, over and over again, each time telling ourselves that now at last we certainly will have the victory, but each time failing even worse than before.

But you may ask, "Are we not to do any fighting ourselves?" Of course we are to fight, but not like this. We are to fight the "good fight of faith," as Paul exhorted Timothy. The fight of faith is not a fight of effort or struggle but of trusting. It is the kind of fight that Hezekiah fought when he and his army marched out to meet their enemy, singing songs of victory as they went, and found all their enemies dead. Our part in this fight is to hand the battle over to the Lord and trust Him for the victory.

We are also to put on His armor, not our

own. The apostle Paul tells us what it is: the belt of truth, the breastplate of righteousness, the preparation of the Gospel of peace on our feet, the helmet of salvation, and the sword of the Spirit, which is the Word of God. But above all, he says, we are to take the shield of faith with which we will be able to quench all the fiery darts of the wicked one (see Ephesians 6:14–16).

There is nothing here about promises or resolutions, nothing about hours and days of agonizing struggles and bitter remorse. "Above all, taking the shield of faith." Above all things, faith. Faith is the one essential thing, without which all else is useless. And it means that we must not only hand the battle over to the Lord, but we must leave it with Him and have absolute faith that He will conquer. It is here that the fight comes in. It seems so unsafe to sit still and do nothing but trust the Lord, and the temptation to take the battle back into our own hands is often tremendous. To keep our hands off in spiritual matters is as hard for us as it is for a drowning man to keep his hands off the one who is trying to rescue him. We all know how impossible it is to rescue a drowning man who tries to help his rescuer, and it is equally impossible for the Lord to fight our battles for us when we insist on trying to fight them ourselves. It is not that He will not, but He cannot. Our interference hinders His working. Spiritual forces cannot work while earthly forces are active.

Our Lord tells us that without Him we can do nothing, and we have read and repeated His words hundreds of times, but does anyone really believe they are actually true? If we should drag out into the light our secret thoughts on the subject, wouldn't we find them to be something like this: "When Christ said those words He meant, of course, to say that we cannot of ourselves do much, or at any rate no great things. But nothing? No, that is impossible. We are not babies, and we are certainly meant to use all the strength we have in fighting our enemies. And when our own strength gives out, we can then call upon the Lord to help us." In spite of all our failures, we cannot help thinking that, if only we should try harder and be more persistent, we should be equal to any encounter. But we entirely overlook the vital fact that our natural powers are of no avail in spiritual regions or with spiritual enemies. They are, in fact, real hindrances, just as trying to walk would hinder us if we sought to float or fly. The result of trusting in ourselves, then, when dealing with our spiritual enemies must be very serious. It not only causes failure, but in the end it causes rebellion, and a great deal of what is called "spiritual conflict" might far better be named "spiritual rebellion." God has told us to cease from our own efforts and to hand our battles over to Him, but we point-blank refuse to obey Him. We fight, it is true, but it is not a fight of faith but a fight of unbelief. Our spiritual "wrestling," of which we are often so proud, is really a wrestling, not for God against His enemies, but against Him on the side of His enemies. We allow ourselves to indulge in doubts and fears, and as a consequence we are plunged into darkness, turmoil, and wrestling of spirit. And then we call this "spiritual conflict" and look upon ourselves as an interesting and "peculiar case." The single word that explains our "peculiar case" is the word *unbelief*, and the simple remedy is to be found in the word *faith*.

But, you may ask, what about "wrestling Jacob"? Did he not gain his victory by wrestling? On the contrary, he gained his victory by being made so weak that he could not wrestle any longer. It was not Jacob who wrestled with the angel, but the angel who wrestled with Jacob. Jacob was the one to be overcome; and when the angel found that Jacob's resistance was so great that he could not "prevail against him," he was forced to make him lame by putting his thigh out of joint. Then the victory was won. As soon as Jacob was too weak to resist any longer, he prevailed with God. He gained power when he lost it. He conquered when he could no longer fight.

Jacob's experience is ours. The Lord wrestles with us in order to bring us to a place of entire dependence on Him. We resist as long as we have any strength, until at last He is forced to bring us to a place of helplessness, where we are obliged to yield, and then we conquer by this very yielding. Our victory is always the victory of weakness. Paul knew this victory when he said: "And He said to me, 'My grace is sufficient for you, for My strength is made perfect in weakness.' Therefore most gladly I will rather boast in my infirmities, that the power of Christ may rest upon me. Therefore I take pleasure in infirmities, in reproaches, in needs, in persecutions, in distresses, for Christ's sake. For when I am weak, then I am strong" (2 Corinthians 12:9–10).

Who would ask for a more magnificent victory than this!

And this victory will be ours, if we take the Lord to be our Banner and commit all our battles to Him.

The name of Jehovah-shalom, or "the Lord our peace," was discovered by Gideon when the Lord had called him to a work he felt himself to be completely unfit for. "O my Lord," he had said, "how can I save Israel? Indeed my clan is the weakest in Manasseh, and I am the least in my father's house" (Judges 6:15). The Lord answered him, saying, "Surely I will be with you, and you shall defeat the Midianites as one man. . . . Then the LORD said to him, 'Peace be with you; do not fear, you shall not die" (Judges 6:16, 23). Then Gideon believed the Lord, and although the battle had not yet been fought and no victories had been won, with the eye of faith he saw peace already secured and he built an altar to the Lord, calling it Jehovah-shalom, "the Lord our peace."

Of all the needs of the human heart, none is greater than the need for peace, and none is more abundantly promised in the Gospel. "Peace I leave with you," says our Lord, "My peace I give to you. . . . Let not your heart be troubled, neither let it be afraid" (John 14:27). And again He says: "These things I have spoken to you, that in Me you may have peace. In the world you will have tribulation; but be of good cheer, I have overcome the world" (John 16:33).

Our idea of peace is that it must be outward before it can be inward, that all enemies must be driven away and all troubles cease. But the Lord's idea was of an interior peace that could exist in the midst of turmoil and triumph over it. The ground for this sort of peace is found in the fact that Christ has overcome the world. Only the conqueror can proclaim peace, and the people, whose battles He has fought, can do nothing but enter into it. They can neither make nor unmake it. But if they choose, they can refuse to believe in it and so fail to let it reign in their hearts. You may be afraid to believe that Christ has made peace for you, but He has done it, and all your continued warfare is worse than useless.

The Bible tells us that Christ is our peace, and consequently, whether I feel as if I have peace or not, peace is really mine in Christ and I must take possession of it by faith. Faith is simply to believe and assert the thing that God says. If He says there is peace, faith asserts that there is and enters into the enjoyment of it.

We can always enter into peace by a simple obedience to Philippians 4:6–7: "Be anxious for nothing, but in everything by prayer and supplication, with thanksgiving, let your requests be made known to God; and the peace of God, which surpasses all understanding, will guard your hearts and minds through Christ Jesus." The steps here are very plain, and they are only two. First, give up all anxiety; and second, hand over your cares to God. Then stand strong here; peace must come.

The name Jehovah-tsidkenu, "the Lord our righteousness," was revealed by the Lord Himself through the mouth of the prophet Jeremiah when he was announcing the coming of Christ. "'Behold, the days are coming,' says the LORD, 'that I will raise to David a Branch of righteousness; a King shall reign and prosper, and execute judgment and righteousness in the earth. In his days Judah will be saved, and Israel will dwell safely; now this is His name by which He will be called: THE LORD OUR RIGHTEOUSNESS'" (Jeremiah 23:5–6).

Most of the struggles and conflicts of our Christian life come from our fights with sin and our efforts after righteousness. And I need not say how great are our failures. As long as we try to conquer sin or attain righteousness by our own efforts, we are bound to fail. But if we discover that the Lord is our righteousness, we will have the secret of victory. In the Lord Jesus Christ we have a fuller revelation of this wonderful name of God. The apostle Paul in his character as the "ambassador for Christ" declares that God has made Christ to be sin for us, that we might become the righteousness of God in Him (see 2 Corinthians 5:21). And again he says that Christ became for us wisdom and righteousness and sanctification and redemption (see 1 Corinthians 1:30).

To me this name of God, the Lord our righteousness, seems of such tremendously practical use that I want to make it plain to others. But it is difficult, and I cannot possibly explain it theologically. But experientially it seems to me like this: We are not to try to have a storehouse of righteousness laid up in ourselves from which to draw a supply when needed, but we are to draw continual fresh supplies as we need them from the righteousness that is laid up for us in Christ.

If we need righteousness of any sort, such as patience, humility, or love, it is useless for us to look within, hoping to find a supply there, for we never will find it; but we must simply take it by faith, as a possession that is stored up for us in Christ, who is our righteousness. I have seen sweetness and gentleness poured like a flood of sunshine into dark and bitter spirits when the hand of faith has been reached out to grasp them as a present possession. I have seen sharp tongues made tender, anxious hearts made calm, and fretful spirits made quiet by the simple step of taking by faith the righteousness that is ours in Christ.

The apostle Paul wrote, "But now the righteousness of God apart from the law is revealed, being witnessed by the Law and the Prophets, even the righteousness of God, through faith in Jesus Christ, to all and on all who believe. For there is no difference" (Romans 3:21–22).

It is faith and faith only that can appropriate this righteousness that is ours in Christ. Just as we appropriate by faith the forgiveness that is ours in Christ, so must we appropriate by faith the patience that is ours in Him, or the gentleness, the meekness, long-suffering, or any other virtue we may need. Our own efforts will not procure righteousness for us, any more than they will procure forgiveness. And yet how many Christians try! Paul describes them when he says: "For I bear them witness that they have a zeal for God, but not according to knowledge. For they being ignorant of God's righteousness, and seeking to establish their own righteousness, have not submitted to the righteousness of God. For Christ is the end of the law for righteousness to everyone who believes" (Romans 10:2–4).

The prophet Isaiah tells us that our own righteousness, even if we could attain to any, is nothing but filthy rags; and Paul prays that he may be found in Christ, not having his own righteousness, which is from the law, but that which is through faith in Christ, the righteousness which is from God by faith (see Philippians 3:9).

Do we comprehend the meaning of this

prayer? And are we prepared to join in it with our whole hearts? If so, our struggle after righteousness will be over. Jehovah-tsidkenu will supply all our needs.

The name Jehovah-shammah, or "the Lord is there," was revealed to the prophet Ezekiel when he was shown by a vision during the twenty-fifth year of their captivity what was to be the future home of the children of Israel. He described the land and the city of Jerusalem, and ended his description by saying: "And the name of the city from that day shall be: THE LORD IS THERE" (Ezekiel 48:35).

To me this name includes all the others. Wherever the Lord is, all must go right for His children. Where the good mother is, all goes right, up to the measure of her ability, for her children. And how much more with God. His presence is enough. We can all remember how the simple presence of our mothers was enough for us when we were children. All that we needed of comfort, rest, and deliverance was ensured to us by the mere fact of our mother, as she sat in her usual chair with her work or her book or her writing, and we had burst in on her with our childish woes. If we could only see that the presence of God is the same assurance of comfort, rest, and deliverance, only infinitely more so, a fountain of joy would be opened up in our lives that would drive out every remnant of discomfort and distress.

All through the Old Testament the Lord's one universal answer to all the fears and anxieties of the children of Israel was the simple words "I will be with you." He did not need to say anything more. His presence was to them a perfect guarantee that all their needs would be supplied.

You may say, "If the Lord would only say the same thing to me, I wouldn't be afraid either." Well, He has said it, and has said it in unmistakable terms. When the angel of the Lord announced to Joseph the coming birth of Christ, he said: "They shall call his name Emmanuel, which is translated, 'God with us.'" In this short sentence is revealed to us the grandest fact the world can ever know—that God, the Almighty God, the creator of heaven and earth, is not a far-off God, dwelling in a heaven of unapproachable glory, but has come down in Christ to dwell with us right here in this world.

Both these names, Jehovah-shammah and Emmanuel, mean the same thing. They mean that God is everywhere present in His universe, surrounding everything, sustaining everything, and holding all of us safe in His care. They mean that we can find no place in all His universe of which it cannot be said, "The Lord is there." The psalmist says, "Where can I go from Your Spirit? Or where can I flee from Your presence? If I ascend into heaven, You are there; if I make my bed in hell, behold, You are there. If I take the wings of the morning, and dwell in the uttermost parts of the sea, even there Your hand shall lead me, and Your right hand shall hold me" (Psalm 139:7–10).

We cannot drift from the love and care of an ever-present God. And those Christians who think He has forsaken them and who cry out for His presence are ignorant of the fact that He is always present with them.

They cannot get out of His presence, even if they tried.

We may never have dreamed that God was such a God as this, and we may have gone all our lives starved, weary, and wretched. But all the time we have been starving in the midst of plenty. The fullness of God's salvation has awaited our faith, and "abundance of grace and of the gift of righteousness" have awaited our receiving.

I hope that from now on you will see that these all-embracing names of God leave no tiny corner of your need unsupplied. Then will you be able to testify with the prophet Isaiah to everyone around you: "Behold, God is my salvation, I will trust and not be afraid; 'for YAH, the LORD, is my strength and song; He also has become my salvation.' Therefore with joy you will draw water from the wells of salvation" (Isaiah 12:2–3).

7

SELF-EXAMINATION

*Examine yourselves as to
whether you are in the faith.*

2 CORINTHIANS 13:5

Probably no subject connected with the religious life has been the cause of more discomfort and suffering to tender consciences than self-examination. And yet it has been so constantly impressed upon us that it is our duty to examine ourselves that our gaze is continually turned inward on our own state and feelings to such an extent that self, and not Christ, fills the whole horizon.

By *self* I mean all that centers around this

great big "me" of ours. We are all familiar with its vocabulary—"I," "me," "my." The questions we ask ourselves in our times of self-examination are proof of this. *Am I earnest enough? Have I repented enough? Have I the right sort of feelings? Do I realize religious truth as I ought? Are my prayers fervent enough? Is my interest in religious things as great as it ought to be? Do I love God with enough fervor? Is the Bible as much of a delight to me as it is to others?* All these and a hundred more questions about ourselves and our experiences fill up all our thoughts, to the utter exclusion of any thought concerning Christ.

Many of us know the misery of this all too well. But the idea that the Bible is full of commands to self-examination is so prevalent that it seems one of the most truly pious things we can do. And miserable as it makes us, we still feel it is our duty to go on with it in spite of an ever-increasing sense of hopelessness and despair.

In view of this idea many will be surprised to find that there are only two texts in the whole Bible that speak of self-examination, and neither of them say anything about the morbid self-analysis that results from what we call self-examination.

One of these passages I have quoted at the beginning of this chapter: "Examine yourselves as to whether you are in the faith." It does not say examine whether you are sufficiently earnest, or whether you have the right feelings, or whether your motives are pure, but simply whether you are "in the faith." In short, do you believe in Christ or do you not?

The other passage reads: "Therefore whoever eats this bread or drinks this cup of the Lord in an unworthy manner will be guilty of the body and blood of the Lord. But let a man examine himself, and so let him eat of the bread and drink of the cup" (1 Corinthians 11:27–28). Paul was writing about the abuses of greediness and drunkenness that had crept in at the celebration of the Lord's Supper, and in this exhortation to examine themselves, he was simply urging them to see that they did none of these things but partook of this religious feast in a decent and orderly manner.

In neither of these passages is there

any hint of the morbid searching of one's emotions and experiences that we call self-examination. The truth is, there is no scriptural authority for this disease of modern times. Some of my readers, however, are probably asking themselves whether I have overlooked a large class of passages that tells us to "watch" and whether these passages don't mean watching ourselves, or, in other words, self-examination. I will quote one of these passages as a sample so we may see what their meaning really is. "But of that day and hour no one knows, not even the angels in heaven, nor the Son, but only the Father. Take heed, watch and pray; for you do not know when the time is. It is like a man going to a far country, who left his house and gave authority to his servants, and to each his work, and commanded the doorkeeper to watch. Watch therefore, for you do not know when the master of the house is coming—in the evening, at midnight, at the crowing of the rooster, or in the morning—lest, coming suddenly, he find you sleeping. And what I say to you, I say to all: Watch!" (Mark 13:32–37).

If we carefully examine this passage and others like it, we will see that instead of teaching self-examination, they teach something exactly the opposite. They tell us to "watch," it is true, but they do not tell us to watch ourselves. They are plainly commands to forget ourselves in watching for Another. The return of the Lord is the thing we are to watch for. His coming footsteps, and not our own past footsteps, are to be the object of our gazing.

"Blessed are those servants whom the master, when he comes, will find watching" (Luke 12:37). Watching what? Themselves? No, watching for Him, of course. If we can imagine a porter, instead of watching for the return of his master, spending his time morbidly analyzing his own past conduct, trying to discover whether he had been faithful enough and becoming so absorbed in self-examination that he doesn't hear the master's call and misses the master's return, we will have a picture of what goes on in the soul that is given up to the mistaken habit of watching and looking at self instead of watching and looking for Christ.

God says, "Look to Me and you will be saved," but the self-analyzing soul says, "I must look to myself if I am to have any hope of being saved. It must be by getting myself right that salvation is to come." We see what we look at and cannot see what we look away from, and we cannot look to Jesus while we are looking at ourselves. The power for victory and endurance are to come from looking to Jesus and considering Him. Looking at ourselves causes weakness and defeat. The reason is that when we look at ourselves, we see nothing but ourselves and our own weakness, poverty, and sin. We do not and cannot see the remedy and the supply for these, and we are defeated. The remedy and the supply are there all the time, but they are not to be found in the place where we are looking, for they are not in self but in Christ; and we cannot be looking at ourselves and looking at Christ at the same time.

The Bible law in regard to the self-life is not that the self-life must be watched and made better, but that it must be "put off." The apostle, when urging the Ephesian

Christians to walk worthy of their calling, tells them that they must "put off" the old man, which is corrupt according to deceitful lusts. The "old man" is, of course, the self-life, and this self-life is not to be improved but to be "put off." It is to be crucified. Paul says that our old man is crucified with Christ, and he declares of the Colossians that they could no longer lie, since they had "put off the old man with his deeds." Some people's idea of crucifying the "old man" is to set him up on a pinnacle and then walk around him and stick nagging pins into him to make him miserable, but keeping him alive all the time. But, if I understand language, crucifixion means death, not making miserable; and to crucify the old man means to kill him outright and to put him off as a snake puts off its dead and useless skin.

It is of no use, then, for us to examine self and tinker with it in the hope of improving it, for the thing the Lord wants us to do with it is to get rid of it. The only safe and scriptural way is to have nothing to do with self at all, to ignore it altogether, and to fix our eyes, our thoughts, and our expectations on the Lord and on Him alone. We must substitute for the personal pronouns "I," "me," "my" the pronouns "He," "Him," "His"; and must ask ourselves, not "am I good?" but "is He good?"

The psalmist says: "My eyes are ever toward the LORD, for he shall pluck my feet out of the net" (Psalm 25:15). As long as our eyes are looking at our own feet, and the net in which they're entangled, we only get into worse tangles. But when we keep our eyes on the Lord, He plucks our feet out of the net. This is a practical experience I have tested hundreds of times, and I know it is a fact. No matter what sort of a snarl I may have been in, whether inward or outward, I have always found that while I kept my eyes on the snarl and tried to unravel it, it grew worse and worse; but when I turned my eyes away from the snarl and kept them fixed on the Lord, He always sooner or later unraveled it and delivered me.

Have you ever watched a farmer plowing a field? If you have, you will have noticed that in order to make straight furrows he must fix his eyes on a tree or a post in the fence or some object at the farther end of the field, and guide his plow unwaveringly toward that object. If he begins to look back at the furrow behind him to see whether he has made a straight furrow, his plow begins to jerk from side to side and the furrow he is making becomes a zigzag. If we would make straight paths for our feet we must do what the apostle Paul says he did. We must forget the things that are behind, and reaching forward to those that are ahead, we must press toward the goal for the prize of the upward call of God in Christ Jesus (see Philippians 3:13–14).

To forget the things that are behind is an essential part of the pressing forward toward the prize of our upward call, and this prize can never be reached unless we consent to this forgetting. When we do consent to it, we come near to putting an end to all our self-examination.

We complain of spiritual hunger and wonder why our hunger is not satisfied. The psalmist says: "The eyes of all look expectantly to You, and You give them their food in due season" (Psalm 145:15). Having our eyes on ourselves and on our own hunger will never bring a supply of spiritual meat. To examine self is to be like a starving man who spends his time examining his empty cupboard instead of going to the market for groceries to fill it. No wonder such Christians seem to be starving to death in the midst of all the fullness there is for them in Christ. They never see that fullness, for they never look at it.

Somehow people seem to lay aside their common sense when they come to the subject of religion and expect to see things they've deliberately kept their backs turned toward. They cry out, "O Lord, reveal Yourself," but instead of looking at Him they look at themselves and their own feelings, and then wonder why God hides His face from their fervent prayers. But how can they see what they don't look at?

It is never God who hides His face from us, but it is always we who hide our face from Him, turning our backs to Him rather than our faces. The prophet Jeremiah reproached the children of Israel for this, adding that they "set their abominations in the house which is called by [God's] name" (Jeremiah 7:30). When Christians spend their time examining their own condition, raking up all their sins, and bemoaning their shortcomings, what is it but setting up the "abomination" of their own sinful self upon the throne of their hearts and making it the center of their whole religious life. They gaze at this great, big, miserable self until it fills their whole horizon, and they "turn their back" on the Lord until He is lost sight of altogether.

One look at Christ is worth more for salvation than a million looks at self. Yet so mistaken are our ideas, we seem unable to avoid thinking that the mortification that results from self-examination must have in it some saving power, because it makes us so miserable. For we have to travel a long way on our heavenly journey before we fully learn that there is no saving power in misery, and that a cheerful, confident faith is the only successful attitude for the aspiring soul.

In Isaiah we see God's people complaining

because they fasted and He did not see, they afflicted their souls and He took no knowledge. God gave them this significant answer: "Is it a fast that I have chosen, a day for a man to afflict his soul? Is it to bow down his head like a bulrush, and to spread out sackcloth and ashes? Would you call this a fast, and an acceptable day to the LORD?" (Isaiah 58:5). Whoever else is pleased with the miseries of our self-examination, it is very certain that God is not. He does not want us to bow our heads like a reed, and He calls upon us to forget our own miserable selves and to work to lessen the miseries of others. "Is this not the fast that I have chosen," He says, "to loose the bonds of wickedness, to undo the heavy burdens, to let the oppressed go free, and that you break every yoke? Is it not to share your bread with the hungry, and that you bring to your house the poor who are cast out; when you see the naked that you cover him?" (Isaiah 58:6–7).

He has shown us here the surest way of deliverance out of the pit of misery that our habits of self-examination have plunged us into. He declares emphatically that if we will only keep the sort of "fast" He approves of, by giving up our own "fast" of afflicting our souls and instead extending our souls to the hungry and trying to bear the burdens and relieve the miseries of others, then our light shall dawn in the darkness, and our darkness be as the noonday. The Lord will guide us continually, satisfying our souls in drought and strengthening our bones; we shall be like a watered garden, and like a spring of water whose waters do not fail (see Isaiah 58:10–11).

Now let us try God's fast. Let us lay aside all care for ourselves and care instead for our needy brothers and sisters. Let us stop trying to do something for our own poor miserable self-life, and begin to try to do something to help the spiritual lives of others. Let us give up our hopeless efforts to find something in ourselves to delight in, and delight ourselves only in the Lord and in His service. If we will do this, the days of our misery will be ended.

But some may ask whether it is still necessary to examine ourselves in order to find out what is wrong and what needs fixing. This would, of course, be necessary if we were our own workmanship, but since we are God's workmanship and not our own, He is the One to examine us, for He is the only One who can tell what is wrong. Surely we must see that the examining of the Lord is the only kind of examination that is of any use. His examination is like that of a physician who examines in order to cure, while our self-examination is like that of the patient who only becomes more of a hypochondriac the more he examines the symptoms of his disease.

But the question may be asked whether, when there has been actual sin, there ought not to be self-examination and self-reproach at least for a time. This is a fallacy that deceives many. It seems too much to believe that we can be forgiven without first going through a season of self-reproach. But what is the Bible teaching? John tells us that if we confess our sins (not mourn over them or try to excuse them), He is faithful and just to forgive us our sins and to cleanse us from all unrighteousness (see 1 John 1:9). All that God wants is that we turn to Him immediately, acknowledge our sin, and believe in His forgiveness. Every minute that we delay doing this to spend time in self-examination and self-reproach is only adding further sin to that which we have already committed. If ever we need to look away from self and have our eyes turned to the Lord, it is just when we become conscious of having sinned against Him. The greater the multitude of our enemies, the greater and more immediate our need of God.

All through the Bible we are taught this lesson of death to self and life in Christ alone. "Not I, but Christ" was not intended to be a unique experience of Paul's but was simply a declaration of what ought to be the experience of every Christian. We sing sometimes "You, O Christ, are all I want," but we really want a great many other things. We want good feelings, we want fervor and earnestness, we want realizations, we want satisfying experiences; and we continually examine ourselves to try to find out why we don't have these things. We think if we could only discover our points of failure, we'd be able to set them straight. But there is no healing or transforming power in gazing at our failures. The only road to Christlikeness is to behold His goodness and beauty. We grow like what we look at, and if we spend our lives looking at our hateful selves, we will become more and more hateful. Looking at self, we are more and more changed into the image of self. While on the contrary, if we spend our time letting our minds dwell on God's goodness and love and trying to drink in His Spirit, the inevitable result will be that we will be changed into the image of the Lord.

We should never indulge in any self-reflective acts, either of shame at our failures or of congratulation at our successes, but we should continually consign self and all self's doings to oblivion and keep our eyes on the Lord. It is very hard in self-examination not to try to find excuses for our faults; and our self-reflective acts are often in danger of being turned into self-glorying ones. They always do harm and never good.

One of the most effective ways to conquer the habit is to make a rule that, whenever we are tempted to examine ourselves, we will immediately begin to examine the Lord instead and let thoughts of His love and His all-sufficiency sweep out all thoughts of our own unworthiness or helplessness.

What we must do is shut the door resolutely upon self and all of self's experiences and to say with the psalmist: "I have set the LORD [not self] always before me; because He is at my right hand I shall not be moved. Therefore my heart is glad, and my glory rejoices: my flesh also will rest in hope" (Psalm 16:8–9).

8

THINGS THAT CANNOT BE SHAKEN

*Now this, 'Yet once more,' indicates the
removal of those things that are being shaken,
as of things that are made, that the things
which cannot be shaken may remain.*

HEBREWS 12:27

After everything we have been considering
about the unfathomable love and care of God,
it might seem to those who don't understand
the deepest ways of love that no trials or
hardship could ever come into the lives of
His children. But if we look deeply into the
matter, we will see that often love itself must

bring the hardships. "Whom the LORD loves He chastens, and scourges every son whom He receives. If you endure chastening, God deals with you as with sons; for what son is there whom a father does not chasten? But if you are without chastening, of which all have become partakers, then you are illegitimate and not sons" (Hebrews 12:6–8).

If love sees those it loves going wrong, it must, because of its very love, do what it can to save them. The love that fails to do this is only selfishness. Therefore, because of His unfathomable love, the God of love, when He sees His children resting their souls on things that can be shaken, must remove those things from their lives in order that they may be driven to rest only on the things that cannot be shaken. And this process of removing is sometimes very hard.

If our souls are to rest in peace and comfort, it can only be on unshakable foundations. To be reliable, foundations must always be unshakable. The house of the foolish man, which is built on the sand, may present a fine appearance in clear and sunshiny weather; but when storms arise, the winds blow, and floods come, that house will fall, and great will be the fall of it. The wise man's house, on the contrary, which is built on the rock, is able to withstand all the stress of the storm, and remains unshaken through winds and floods, for it is "founded on the rock."

It is very possible in the Christian life to build one's spiritual house on such insecure foundations that when storms beat upon it, the ruin of that house is great. Many a religious experience that has seemed fair enough when all was going well in life has tottered and fallen when trials have come, because its foundations have been insecure. It is therefore of vital importance to each one of us to see to it that our religious life is built upon "things that cannot be shaken."

Of course the immediate thought that will come to every mind is that it must be "built upon the rock Christ Jesus." This is true, but the great point is what is meant by that expression. It is one of those religious phrases that is often used with no definite or real meaning attached to it. Conventionally we believe that Christ is the only Rock upon which to build, but practically, we believe that in order to have a rock upon which it will be really safe to build, many other things must be added to Christ. We think, for instance, that the right feelings must be added, or the right doctrines or dogmas, or whatever else may seem to each one of us to constitute the necessary degree of security. And if we were perfectly honest with ourselves, I suspect we should often find that our dependence was almost wholly upon these additions of our own, and that Christ Himself was of secondary importance.

What we ought to mean when we talk about building on the Rock Christ Jesus is that the Lord is enough for our salvation, just the Lord without any additions of our own, the Lord Himself, as He is in His own intrinsic character, our Creator and Redeemer, and our all-sufficient portion.

The "solid foundation of God stands" (2 Timothy 2:19), and it is the only foundation that does. Therefore, we need to be "shaken" off every other foundation in order that we may be forced to rest on the foundation of God alone. And this explains the necessity for those "shakings" so many Christians seem called to pass through. The Lord sees that they are building their spiritual houses on flimsy foundations that will not be able to withstand the violent beating of the storms of life, and not in anger but in tenderest love He shakes our earth and our heaven until all that "can be shaken" is removed, and only those "things that cannot be shaken" are left behind. The writer of Hebrews tells us that the things that are shaken are the "things that are made" (Hebrews 12:27), that is, the things that are manufactured by our own efforts, feelings that we conjure up, doctrines that we elaborate, good works that we perform. It is not that these things are bad things in themselves. It is only when the soul begins to rest on them instead of on the Lord that He is compelled to "shake" us from off them.

There may be times in our religious lives when our experience seems to us as settled and immovable as the roots of the everlasting mountains. But then an upheaval comes and all our foundations are shaken and thrown down, and we are ready to despair and question whether we can be Christians at

all. Sometimes it is an upheaval in our outward circumstances, and sometimes it is in
our inward experience. If people have rested
on their good work and their faithful service,
the Lord is often obliged to take away all
power for work or else all opportunity in
order that the soul may be driven from its
false resting place and forced to rest in the
Lord alone. Sometimes the dependence is on
good feelings or virtuous emotions, and the
soul has to be deprived of these before it can
learn to depend only on God. Sometimes it
is upon "sound doctrine" that the dependence is placed, and the man feels himself
to be occupying an invulnerable position
because his views are so correct; and then the
Lord is obliged to shake his doctrines and
to plunge him into confusion and darkness
about his views.

Or it may be that the upheaval comes in
our outward circumstances. Everything has
seemed so firmly established in prosperity
that no dream of disaster disturbs us. Our
reputation is assured, our work has pros-
pered, our efforts have all been successful
beyond our hopes, and our soul is at ease; the

need for God is in danger of becoming far off and vague. And then the Lord is obliged to put an end to it all, our prosperity crumbles around us like a house built on sands, and we are tempted to think He is angry with us. But in truth it is not anger but most tender love. His very love is what compels Him to take away the outward prosperity that is keeping our souls from entering into the interior spiritual kingdom for which we long. When the fig tree stops blossoming and there is no fruit on the vines; when the labor of the olive fails and the fields yield no food; when the flock is cut off from the fold and there is no herd in the stalls, then, and often not until then, will our souls learn to rejoice in the Lord only, and to joy in the God of our salvation (see Habakkuk 3:17–18).

Paul declared that he counted all things but loss that he might win Christ; and when we learn to say the same, the peace and joy that the Gospel promises become our permanent possession.

"What injustice," asks the Lord of the children of Israel, "have your fathers found in Me, that they have gone far from Me, have

followed idols, and have become idolaters?
. . . For my people have committed two evils:
they have forsaken Me, the fountain of living
waters, and hewn themselves cisterns—
broken cisterns that can hold no water"
(Jeremiah 2:5, 13). Like the Israelites, we too
forsake the fountain of living waters and try
to carve out for ourselves cisterns of our own
devising. We seek to quench our thirst with
our own experiences or our own activities,
and then wonder why we still thirst. And it
is to save us from perishing for lack of water
that the Lord finds it necessary to destroy our
broken cisterns, since only then can we be
forced to drink from the fountain of living
waters.

We are told that if we "trust in vanity,"
vanity will be our reward. Have you ever cros-
sed a dangerous swamp filled with quick-
sands, where every step was a risk and where
firm-looking mounds continually deceived
you into a false dependence, causing you to
sink in the muck and water concealed under
their deceptive appearances? If you have, you
will be able to understand what it means to
"trust in vanity," and you will appreciate the

blessedness of anything that will reveal to you the rottenness of your false dependencies and drive you to trust in what is safe and permanent. When our feet are walking on "miry clay," we can have nothing but welcome for the divine Guide who will bring us out of the clay and "set our feet upon a rock" and "establish our steps," even though the ways in which He calls us to walk may seem narrow and hard (see Psalm 40:2).

The old mystics used to teach what they called "detachment," meaning the cutting loose of the soul from all that could hold it back from God. This need for "detachment" is the secret of many of our "shakings." We cannot follow the Lord fully as long as we are tied to anything else, any more than a boat can sail out into the boundless ocean as long as it is tied to the shore.

If we want to reach the "city that has sure and steadfast foundations," we must go out like Abraham from all other cities and must be detached from every earthly tie. Everything in Abraham's life that could be shaken was shaken. He was, figuratively speaking, emptied from vessel to vessel, here today and gone tomorrow; all his resting places were disturbed, with no settlement or comfort anywhere. We, like Abraham, are looking for a city that has foundations, whose builder and maker is God, and therefore we too will need to be emptied from vessel to vessel. The psalmist had learned this, and after all the shakings and emptying of his eventful life, he cried: "My soul, wait silently for God alone, for my expectation is from Him. He only is my rock and my salvation; He is my defense; I shall not be moved. In God is my salvation and my glory; the rock of my strength, and my refuge, is in God" (Psalm 62:5–7).

At last God was everything to him, and then he found that God was enough.

"Therefore we will not fear, even though the earth be removed, and though the mountains be carried into the midst of the sea; though its waters roar and be troubled, though the mountains shake with its swelling. . . . God is in the midst of her, she shall not be moved. God shall help her, just at the break of dawn" (Psalm 46:2–3, 5). Can it be possible that we, who are so easily moved by the things of earth, can arrive at a place where nothing can upset our temper or disturb our calm? Yes, it is possible, and the apostle Paul knew it. When he was on his way to Jerusalem, where he foresaw that "chains and tribulations" awaited him, he could say triumphantly, "But none of these things move me" (Acts 20:24). Everything in Paul's life and experience that could be shaken had been shaken, and he no longer counted his life, or any of life's possessions, dear to him. And we, if we will let God have His way with us, may come to the same place so that neither the fear of the little things of life nor its trials can have power to move us from the peace that passes all understanding.

"Therefore, since we are receiving a kingdom which cannot be shaken, let us have grace, by which we may serve God acceptably with reverence and godly fear. For our God is a consuming fire" (Hebrews 12:28–29). Many people are afraid of the consuming fire of God, but that is only because they don't understand what it is. It is the fire of God's love that must consume everything that can harm His people; and if our hearts are set on being what the love of God would have us be, His fire is something we won't be afraid of but will warmly welcome.

Let us thank God, then, that the consuming fire of His love won't stop burning until it has refined us as silver is refined. For the promise is that "He will sit as a refiner and a purifier of silver" (Malachi 3:3), and He will purify us as gold and silver are purified in order that we may offer to Him an offering in righteousness. And He gives us this inspiring assurance, that if we will but submit to this purifying process, we will become "pleasant to the LORD" (Malachi 3:4), and all nations will call us blessed, "'for you will be a delightful land,' says the LORD of hosts" (Malachi 3:12).

To be "pleasant" and "delightful" to the Lord may seem to us impossible, when we look at our shortcomings and our unworthiness. But when we think of this lovely, consuming fire of God's love, we can be of good heart and take courage, for He will not fail nor be discouraged until all our dross is burned up and we come forth in His likeness and are conformed to His image.

9

DISCOURAGEMENT

*The soul of the people became
very discouraged on the way.*

NUMBERS 21:4

The church of Christ abounds with people
who are "discouraged on the way." Things
look all wrong and there seems to be no
hope of escape. Their souls faint in them,
and their religious lives are full of misery.
There is nothing that so paralyzes effort as
discouragement, and nothing that more
continually and successfully invites defeat.
The secret of failure or success in any matter
lies far more in the soul's interior attitude

than in any other cause or causes.

And nowhere is this truer than in the spiritual life. The Bible declares that faith is the law of the spiritual life, and that according to our faith it always will be unto us. Then, since faith and discouragement cannot exist together, it is perfectly clear that discouragement must be a barrier to faith. And where discouragement rules, the converse to the law of faith must rule also, and it will be to us, not according to our faith, but according to our discouragement.

An allegory that I heard very early in my Christian life has always remained in my memory. The allegory declared that once upon a time Satan, who desired to ensnare a devoted Christian worker, gathered a council of his helpers to decide on the best way of doing it, and to ask for volunteers. After the case had been explained, an imp offered himself to do the work.

"How will you do it?" asked Satan.

"I will paint for him the delights and pleasures of a life of sin in such glowing colors that he will be eager to enter into it."

"That won't do," said Satan, shaking his head. "The man has tried sin, and he knows better. He knows it leads to misery and ruin, and he will not listen to you."

Then another imp offered himself, and again Satan asked, "What will you do to win the man over?"

"I will picture for him the trials and the self-denials of a righteous life and will make him eager to escape from them."

"Ah, that will not do either," said Satan, "for he has tried righteousness, and he knows that its paths are paths of peace and happiness."

Then a third imp started up and declared that he was sure he could bring the man over.

"Why, what will you do," asked Satan, "that you are so sure?"

"I will discourage his soul," replied the imp triumphantly.

"That will do, that will do!" exclaimed Satan. "You will be successful. Go and bring back your victim."

Discouragement cannot have its source in God. The religion of the Lord Jesus Christ is a religion of faith, of good cheer, of courage, of hope that doesn't disappoint. "Be discouraged," says our lower nature, "for the world is a place of temptation and sin." "Be of good cheer," says Christ, "for I have over come the world." There cannot possibly be any room for discouragement in a world that Christ has overcome.

We must settle it then that discouragement comes from an evil source, only and always.

The causes for our discouragement seem so legitimate that to be discouraged seems to our shortsightedness the only right and proper state of mind to cultivate. The first and perhaps the most common of these causes is the fact of our own incapacity. It is right for us to be cast down, we think, because we know ourselves to be such poor, miserable, good-for-nothing creatures.

Moses is an illustration of this. The Lord had called him to lead the children of Israel out of the land of Egypt; and Moses, looking at this own natural infirmities and weaknesses, was discouraged and tried to excuse himself: "I am not eloquent. . .but I am slow of speech and slow of tongue. . . . They will not believe me or listen to my voice" (Exodus 4:10, 1). One would think that Moses had plenty of cause for discouragement, but notice how the Lord answered Moses, for in the same way, I am convinced, does He answer us. He did not do what Moses no doubt would have liked best—try to convince him that he really was eloquent or that his tongue was not slow of speech. He simply called attention to the fact that, since He had made man's mouth and would Himself be with the mouth He had made, there could not possibly be any cause for discouragement, even if Moses did have all the infirmities of speech he had complained about. "The LORD said to him, Who has made man's mouth? Or who makes the mute, the deaf, the seeing, or the blind? Have not I, the LORD? Now therefore, go, and I will be with your mouth and teach you what you shall say" (Exodus 4:11–12).

Gideon is another illustration. The Lord had called him to undertake the deliverance of His people from the oppression of the Midianites and had said to him: "Go in this might of yours, and you shall save Israel from the hand of the Midianites. Have I not sent you?" (Judges 6:14). This ought to have been enough for Gideon, but he was a poor, unknown man of no family or position and no apparent aptitude for such a great mission. He naturally became discouraged and said: "How can I save Israel? Indeed my clan is the weakest in Manasseh, and I am the least in my father's house" (Judges 6:15). Other men, he felt, who had power and influence might perhaps accomplish this great work, but not one so poor and insignificant as himself. How familiar this sort of talk must sound to the victims of discouragement among my readers, and how sensible and reasonable it seems! But what did the Lord think of it? "And the LORD said to him, 'Surely I will be with you, and you shall defeat the Midianites as one man'" (Judges 6:16). Not one word of encouragement did He give Gideon but merely the statement "I will be with you." To all words of discouragement in the Bible this is the invariable answer, "I will be with you," and it is an answer that precludes all possibility of argument or of any further discouragement. I your Creator and Redeemer, your strength and wisdom, your omnipresent and omniscient God, I will be with you and will protect you through everything. No enemy shall hurt you, no strife of tongues shall disturb you; My presence shall be your safety and your sure defense.

Discouragement comes in many subtle forms, and our spiritual enemies attack us in many disguises. Our own particular makeup or temperament is one of the most common and insidious of our enemies. Other people who are made differently can be cheerful and courageous, we think, but it is right that we should be discouraged when we see the sort of people we are. And there would indeed be ample cause for discouragement if we were to be called upon to fight our battles ourselves. But if the Lord is to fight them for us, it puts an entirely different spin on the matter, and our lack of ability to fight becomes an advantage instead of a disadvantage. We can only be strong in Him when we are weak in ourselves, and our weakness, therefore, is in reality our greatest strength.

The children of Israel can give us a warning lesson here. After the Lord had delivered them out of Egypt and had brought them to the borders of the promised land, Moses urged them to go up and possess it. "Look," he said, "the LORD your God has set the land before you; go up and possess it, as the LORD God of your fathers has spoken to you; do not fear or be discouraged" (Deuteronomy 1:21). But the circumstances were so discouraging and they felt themselves to be so helpless that they could not believe God would really do all He had said, so they murmured in their tents and declared that it must be because the Lord hated them that He had brought them out of Egypt in order to deliver them into the hands of their enemies. And they said, "Where can we go up? Our brethren have discouraged our hearts, saying, 'The people are greater and taller than we; the cities are great and fortified up to heaven; moreover we have seen the sons of the Anakim there'" (Deuteronomy 1:28).

When we read the report of the spies we cannot be surprised at their discouragement. "'The land through which we have gone as spies,'" the spies declared, "'is a land that devours its inhabitants, and all the people whom we saw in it are men of great stature. There we saw the giants. . .and we were like grasshoppers in our own sight, and so we were in their sight'" (Numbers 13:32–33). We also often feel ourselves to be but grasshoppers in the face of the giants of temptation and trouble that attack us, and we think ourselves justified in being discouraged. But the question is not whether we are grasshoppers but whether God is, for it is not we who have to fight these giants but God.

In vain Moses reminded the Israelites of this truth. In vain he assured them that they had no need to be afraid of even the sons of the Anakims, for the Lord their God would fight for them. He even reminded them of past deliverances and asked them if they didn't remember how that "in the wilderness where you saw how the LORD your God carried you, as a man carries his son, in all the way that you went" (Deuteronomy 1:31); but they were still too discouraged to believe. And the result was that not one of that generation was allowed to see the Promised Land, except Caleb and Joshua, who had steadfastly believed that God could and would lead them in.

Such are the fruits of giving way to discouragement, and such is the reward of a steadfast faith.

In commenting on this story, the writer of Hebrews said, "And to whom did He swear that they would not enter His rest, but to those who did not obey? So we see that they could not enter in because of unbelief" (Hebrews 3:18–19).

Do we not look at our weakness instead of the Lord's strength, and have we not sometimes become so discouraged that we cannot even listen to the Lord's own declarations that He will fight for us and will give us the victory? Our souls long to enter into the rest the Lord has promised, but giants and cities great and fortified up to heaven seem to stand in our way, and we are afraid to believe. So we too, like the Israelites, cannot enter in because of unbelief.

How different it would be if we only had enough faith to say with the psalmist: "Though an army may encamp against me, my heart shall not fear; though war may rise against me, in this I will be confident. . . . For in the time of trouble He shall hide me in His pavilion; in the secret place of His tabernacle He shall hide me; He shall set me high upon a rock" (Psalm 27:3, 5).

Another very subtle cause for discouragement is to be found in what is called the fear of man. There seems to exist in this world a company of beings called "they" who lord it over life with an iron hand of control. What will "they" say? What will "they" think? are among the most frequent questions that assail the timid soul when it seeks to work for the Lord. At every turn this omnipotent and ubiquitous "they" stands in our way to discourage us and make us afraid. This form of discouragement is likely to come under the subtle disguise of a due consideration for the opinion of others, but it is especially dangerous because it exalts this "they" into the place of God and esteems "their" opinions above His promises. The only remedy here is simply the reiteration of the fact that God is with us. "'Do not be afraid of their faces, for I am with you to deliver you,' says the LORD." "For He Himself has said, 'I will never leave you nor forsake you.' So we may boldly say, 'The Lord is my helper; I will not fear. What can man do to me?'" (Hebrews 13:5–6).

There is, however, one sort of discouragement that is very common: the discouragement that arises from our own failures. It was from this sort of discouragement that the children of Israel suffered after their defeat at Ai. They had "committed a trespass regarding the accursed things" (Joshua 7:1) and "therefore [they] could not stand before their enemies" (Joshua 7:12). So great was their discouragement that it is said, "Therefore the hearts of the people melted and became like water" (Joshua 7:5) and "Joshua tore his clothes, and fell to the earth on his face before the ark of the LORD until evening, he and the elders of Israel; and they put dust on their heads" (Joshua 7:6). When God's own people "turn their backs before their enemies" one might think discouragement and despair would seem the only proper and safe condition. But evidently the Lord thought otherwise, for He said to Joshua, "Get up! Why do you lie thus on your face?" (Joshua 7:10). The proper thing to do after a failure is not to abandon ourselves to discouragement but to immediately face the evil, get rid of it, and consecrate ourselves once again to the Lord.

But you may ask whether a sense of sin produced by the convictions of the Holy Spirit ought not to cause discouragement. If I see myself to be a sinner, how can I help being discouraged? To this I answer that the Holy Spirit does not convict us of sin in order to discourage us but to encourage us. His work is to show us our sin, not that we may lie down in despair under its power but that we may get rid of it.

Surely then when God says to us, "Though your sins are like scarlet, they shall be as white as snow" (Isaiah 1:18), it is pure unbelief on our part to allow ourselves to be discouraged at even the worst of our failures.

If we could examine the causes of the re-
belling and murmuring thoughts that sometimes fill us, we could find that they always
begin in discouragement. The truth is that
discouragement is really a "speaking against
God," for it implies some sort of a failure on
His part to come up to what His promises
have led us to expect of Him. The psalmist
recognized this and said concerning the discouraging questions His people asked in the
days of their wilderness wandering, "Yes,
they spoke against God: they said, 'Can God
prepare a table in the wilderness?'" (Psalm
78:19). It appears, therefore, that even our
questions as to God's power or willingness to
help us are really a "speaking against God" and
are displeasing to Him, because they reveal
the sad fact that we don't believe in Him and
don't trust in His salvation (see Psalm 78:22).

Another bad thing about discouragement
is its contagiousness. The "bad report" that so
many Christians bring of their failures and
their disappointments in the Christian life is
one of the most discouraging things in our

relationships with one another.

So important did the Lord feel it to be that no one should discourage the heart of another that when Moses was giving the Israelites God's laws concerning their methods of warfare, he said: "The officers shall speak further to the people, and say, 'What man is there who is fearful and fainthearted? Let him go and return to his house, lest the heart of his brethren faint like his heart'" (Deuteronomy 20:8).

We know from experience that courage is contagious and that one really brave soul in moments of danger can save a crowd from a panic. But we too often fail to remember that the converse of this is true, and that one fainthearted man or woman can infect a whole crowd with fear. We consequently think nothing of expressing with the utmost freedom the discouragements that are para-lyzing our own courage.

"Be of good cheer" is the command of the Lord for His disciples, under all circumstances, and He founded this command on the tremendous fact that He had overcome the world (see John 16:33). If we only under-stood what it means that Christ has overcome the world, I believe we would be aghast at the very idea of any of His followers ever be-ing discouraged again.

How different it would be if discourage-ment were looked upon in its true light as a "speaking against God," and only encourag-ing words were permitted among Christians and encouraging reports heard! Who can tell how many spiritual defeats and disasters your discouragements may have brought about in your own life and in the lives of those around you?

In one of Isaiah's prophecies that begins with, "Comfort, yes, comfort My people! says your God" (Isaiah 40:1), he gives us a won-derful description of God as the ground of comfort, and then presents what His people ought to be: "Everyone helped his neighbor, and said to his brother, 'Be of good courage!' So the craftsman encouraged the goldsmith; he who smooths with the hammer inspired him who strikes the anvil" (Isaiah 41:6–7).

If I am asked how we are to get rid of

discouragements, I can only say that we must give them up. It is never worthwhile to argue against discouragement. There is only one argument that can meet it, and that is the argument of God. When David was in the midst of what were perhaps the most discouraging moments of his life, when he had found his city burned and his wives stolen, and he and the men with him had wept until they could weep no more; and when his men, exasperated at their misfortunes, spoke of stoning him, then we are told, "But David encouraged himself in the LORD his God" (1 Samuel 30:6 KJV). The result was a magnificent victory, in which all that they had lost was more than restored to them. This always will be the result of a courageous faith, because faith lays hold of the omnipotence of God.

Over and over the psalmist asks himself this question: "Why are you cast down, O my soul? And why are you disquieted within me?" (Psalm 42:5). And each time he answers himself with the argument of God: "Hope in God, for I shall yet praise Him for the help of

His countenance" (Psalm 42:5). He does not analyze his discouragement or try to argue it away, but he turns at once to the Lord and by faith begins to praise Him.

It is the only way. Discouragement flies where faith appears, and faith flies when discouragement appears. We must choose between them, for they will not mix.

10

❧

THANKSGIVING VERSUS COMPLAINING

In everything give thanks; for this is the will of God in Christ Jesus for you.
1 THESSALONIANS 5:18

Thanksgiving or complaining—these words express two contrasting attitudes of the souls of God's children in regard to His dealings with them, and they are more powerful than we are inclined to believe. The soul that gives thanks can find comfort in everything; the soul that complains can find comfort in nothing.

God's command is "in everything give

thanks," and the command is emphasized by the declaration "for this is the will of God in Christ Jesus for you" (1 Thessalonians 5:18). It is an actual positive command, and if we want to obey God, we simply have to give thanks in everything.

But many Christians have never realized this, and although they may be familiar with the command, they have always seen it as a sort of counsel of perfection mere flesh and blood can never be expected to attain to. And unconsciously, perhaps, they change the wording of the passage to make it say "be resigned" instead of "give thanks," and "in a few things" instead of "in everything," and they leave out altogether the words "for this is the will of God in Christ Jesus for you."

If brought face to face with the actual wording of the command, such Christians will say, "But it's an impossible command. If everything came directly from God, one might do it perhaps, but most things come through human sources and often are the result of sin, and it would not be possible to give thanks for these." To this I answer that it is true we cannot always give thanks for the things themselves, but we can always give thanks for God's love and care in the things. He may not have ordered them, but He is in them somewhere, and He is in them to compel them to work together for our good.

The "second causes" of the wrong may be full of malice and wickedness, but faith never sees second causes. It sees only the hand of God behind the second causes. They are all under His control, and not one of them can touch us except with His knowledge and permission. The thing itself that happens cannot perhaps be said to be the will of God, but by the time its effects reach us they have become God's will for us and must be accepted as from His hands.

The story of Joseph is an illustration of this. Nothing could have seemed more entirely an act of sin nor more utterly contrary to the will of God than his being sold to the Ishmaelites by his wicked brothers, and it would not have seemed possible for Joseph to give thanks. And yet, if he had known the end from the beginning, he would have been filled with thanksgiving. The fact of his having been sold into slavery was the direct doorway to the greatest triumphs and blessings of his life. And, at the end, Joseph himself could say to his wicked brothers: "As for you, you meant evil against me; but God meant it for good" (Genesis 50:20). To the eye of sense it was Joseph's wicked brothers who had sent him into Egypt, but Joseph, looking at it with the eye of faith, said, "God sent me."

We can all remember, I think, similar instances in our own lives when God has made the wrath of man to praise Him and has caused even the hardest trials to work together for our greatest good. I recall once in my own life when a trial was brought on me by another person, at which I was filled with bitter rebellion and could not see in it from beginning to end anything to be thankful for. But that very trial worked out for me the richest blessings and the greatest triumphs of my whole life; and in the end I was filled with thanksgiving for the very things that had caused me such bitter rebellion before. If only I had had faith enough to give thanks at first, how much sorrow would have been spared me.

But I am afraid that the greatest height most Christians in their shortsightedness seem able to rise is to strive after resignation to things they cannot alter and to seek for patience to endure them. The result is that thanksgiving is almost an unknown exercise among the children of God.

Moreover, many not only fail to give thanks but do exactly the opposite and allow themselves instead to complain about God's dealings with them. Instead of looking out for His goodness, they seem to delight in picking out His shortcomings, thinking they show a spirit of discernment in criticizing His laws and His ways.

But complaining is always alike, whether it is on the temporal or the spiritual plane. It always has in it the element of fault finding. Webster says *to complain* means "to make a charge or an accusation." It is not merely disliking the thing we have to bear, but it contains the element of finding fault with the agency that lies behind it. And if we will carefully examine the true nature of our complainings, I think we will generally find they are founded on a subtle fault finding with God. We secretly feel as if He were to blame some how, and almost unconsciously to ourselves, we make mental charges against Him.

On the other hand, thanksgiving always involves praise of the giver. Have you ever noticed how much we are urged in the Bible to "praise the Lord"? It seemed to be almost the principal part of the worship of the Israelites. "Praise the LORD! For it is good to sing praises to our God; for it is pleasant, and praise is beautiful" (Psalm 147:1). I believe, if we should count up, we would find that there are more commands given and more examples set for the giving of thanks "always for all things" than for the doing or the leaving undone of anything else.

It is very evident from the whole teaching of Scripture that the Lord loves to be thanked and praised just as much as we like it. I am sure that it gives Him downright pleasure and that our failure to thank Him for His "good and perfect gifts" wounds His loving heart, just as our hearts are wounded when our loved ones fail to appreciate the benefits we have so enjoyed bestowing on them.

When the apostle Paul was exhorting the Ephesian Christians to be "imitators of God as dear children" (Ephesians 5:1), one of the exhortations he gives in connection with being filled with the Spirit is this: "Giving thanks always for all things to God the Father in the name of our Lord Jesus Christ" (Ephesians 5:20). "Always for all things" is a sweeping expression. It must mean that there can be nothing in our lives that has not in it somewhere a cause for thanksgiving.

The apostle Paul tells us that "every creature of God is good, and nothing is to be refused if it is received with thanksgiving" (1 Timothy 4:4). But it is very hard for us to believe things are good when they don't look so. Often the things God sends into our lives look like curses instead of blessings, and those who have no eyes that can see below surfaces judge only by how things seem outwardly and never see the blessed realities beneath.

But even when we realize that things

come directly from God, we find it very hard to give thanks for what hurts us. Do we not, however, all know what it is to thank a skillful physician for his treatment of our diseases, even though that treatment may have been very severe? And surely we should no less give thanks to our divine Physician when He is obliged to give us bitter medicine to cure our spiritual diseases or perform a painful operation to rid us of something that harms.

But instead of thanking Him we complain against Him, although we generally direct our complaints, not against the divine Physician Himself who has ordered our medicine, but against the "bottle" in which He has sent it. This "bottle" is usually some human being whose unkindness or carelessness or cruelty has caused our suffering but who has been after all only the instrumentality or "second cause" that God has used for our healing.

When the children of Israel found themselves wandering in the wilderness, they "murmured against Moses and Aaron" and complained that they had brought them into the wilderness to kill them with hunger. But in reality their complaining was against God, for it was really He who had brought them there. And the psalmist in recounting the story afterward called this murmuring against Moses and Aaron a "speaking against God."

We may settle it, therefore, that all complaining is "speaking against God." We may think that our discomforts and deprivations have come from human hands only and may therefore feel at liberty to complain, but God is the great Cause behind all second causes. The second causes are only the instruments that He uses, and when we murmur against these, we are really murmuring against God Himself.

The psalmist says: "I will praise the name of God with a song, and will magnify Him with thanksgiving. This also shall please the LORD better than an ox or bull, which has horns and hooves" (Psalm 69:30–31). Many people seem quite ready and willing to offer up some great sacrifice to the Lord but never seem to realize that a little genuine praise and thanksgiving offered to Him now and then would "please Him better" than all their great sacrifices made in His cause.

The Bible is full of this thought from beginning to end. Over and over it is called a "sacrifice of thanksgiving," showing that it is really an act of religious worship. In fact, the "sacrifice of thanksgiving" was one of the regular sacrifices ordained by God in the book of Leviticus. "Oh, that men would give thanks to the LORD for His goodness, and for His wonderful works to the children of men! Let them sacrifice the sacrifices of thanksgiving, and declare His works with rejoicing" (Psalm 107:21–22).

It is such an easy thing to offer the "sacrifice of thanksgiving" that you would think everybody would be eager to do it. But somehow the contrary seems to be the case; and if the prayers of Christians were all to be noted for any one single day, I fear it would be found that with them, as it was with the ten lepers who had been cleansed, nine out of every ten had offered no genuine thanks at all. Our Lord Himself was grieved at these ungrateful lepers and said: "Were there not ten cleansed? But where are the nine? Were there not any found who returned to give glory to God except this foreigner?" (Luke 17: 17–18). Will He have to ask the same question regarding any of us?

Some people are always complaining, nothing ever pleases them, and no kindness seems ever to be appreciated. We know how uncomfortable the company of such people makes us. How often is it despairingly said of fretful, complaining spirits upon whom every care and attention has been lavished, "Will nothing ever satisfy them?" And how often must God turn away, grieved by our complaining, when His love has been lavished on us in untold blessings.

Job was a great complainer, and if ever anyone had good reasons for complaining, he did. His circumstances seemed to be full of hopeless misery. "My soul loathes my life; I will give free course to my complaint; I will speak the bitterness of my soul. I will say to God, 'Do not condemn me; show me why You contend with me. Does it seem good to You that You should oppress, that You should despise the work of Your hands?'" (Job 10:1–3).

We can hardly wonder at Job's complaint. And yet if he could have seen the divine side of all his troubles, he would have known that they were permitted in the tenderest love and were to bring him a revelation of God that he could have had by no other means. If he could have seen that this was to be the outcome he would not have uttered a single complaint but would have given triumphant thanks for the trials that were to bring him such a glorious result. And if we could see, in our heaviest trials, the end from the beginning, I am sure that thanksgiving would take the place of complaining in every case.

The children of Israel were always complaining about something. They complained because they had no water; and when water was supplied they complained that it was bitter to their taste. And we likewise complain because the spiritual water we have to drink seems bitter to our taste. Our souls are thirsty, and we don't like the supply that seems to be provided. Our experiences do not quench our thirst, our religious exercises seem dull and unsatisfying, and we feel ourselves to be in a dry and thirsty land. We have turned from the "Fountain of living waters," and then we complain because the cisterns we have hewn for ourselves hold no water.

The Israelites complained about their food. They had so little confidence in God that they were afraid they would die of starvation; and then when the heavenly manna was provided they complained again because they "loathed such light food." And we also complain about our spiritual food. We have so little confidence in God that we are always afraid we shall die of spiritual starvation. We complain because our preacher does not feed us, or because our religious privileges are very scanty, or because we are not supplied with the same spiritual fare as others are. We have asked God to feed us, and then our souls "loathe" the food He gives and we think it is too "light" to sustain or strengthen us.

If only we knew that the provision our divine Master has made of spiritual drink and spiritual food is just what is best for us. The amazing thing is that we cannot believe now, without waiting for the end, that the

Shepherd knows what pasture is best for His sheep. Surely if we did, our hearts would be filled with thanksgiving and our mouths with praise even in the wilderness.

No depth of misery is too great for the sacrifice of thanksgiving. We cannot give thanks for the misery, but we can give thanks to the Lord in the misery. No matter what our trouble, the Lord is in it somewhere, and He is there to help and bless us.

It is not because things are good that we are to thank the Lord, but because He is good. We are not wise enough to judge whether things are really, in their essence, joys or sorrows. But we always know that the Lord is good and that His goodness makes it absolutely certain that everything He provides or permits must be good.

We are commanded to enter into His gates with thanksgiving and into His courts with praise, and I am convinced that the giving of thanks is the key that opens these gates more quickly than anything else. Try it, dear reader. The next time you feel dead, cold, and depressed, begin to praise and thank the

Lord. Number the benefits He has bestowed on you, thank Him heartily for each one, and see if your spirits don't begin to rise and your heart get warmed up.

I wish I had room to quote all the passages in the Bible about giving thanks and praises to the Lord. There are hundreds and hundreds of them. I beg of you to read the last seven psalms and see what you think. They are full of the things the psalmist calls upon us to give thanks for, all of them relating to the character and ways of God.

The psalmist knew how to count his many blessings, and he would have us do likewise. Try it, and you will indeed be surprised to see what the Lord has done.

The last verse of the book of Psalms, taken in connection with the vision of John in the book of Revelation, is very significant. The psalmist says, "Let everything that has breath praise the LORD" (Psalm 150:6). And in the book of Revelation, John tells us that he heard this being done. "And every creature which is in heaven and on the earth and under the earth and such as are in the sea, and all that are in them, I heard saying, 'Blessing and honor and glory and power be to Him who sits on the throne, and to the Lamb, forever and ever!'" (Revelation 5:13).

The time for universal praise is sure to come someday. Let us begin to do our part now.

11

CONFORMED TO THE IMAGE OF CHRIST

For whom He foreknew, He also predestined to be conformed to the image of His Son, that He might be the firstborn among many brethren.

ROMANS 8:29

God's ultimate purpose in our creation was that we should finally be "conformed to the image of Christ." Christ was to be the firstborn among many brethren, and His brethren were to be like Him. All the discipline and training of our lives is with this end in view, and God has implanted in every human heart a longing, however unformed and unexpressed, after the best and highest it knows.

Christ is the pattern of what each one of us is to be when finished. We are "predestined" to be conformed to His image. We are to be "partakers of the divine nature" (2 Peter 1:4) with Christ; we are to be filled with the spirit of Christ; we are to share His resurrection life and walk as He walked. We are to be one with Him, as He is one with the Father; and the glory God gave to Him, He is to give to us. And when all this is brought to pass, God's purpose in our creation will be fully accomplished and we will stand in His image.

Our likeness to His image is an accomplished fact in the mind of God, but we are, so to speak, still in the factory, and the great master Workman is at work on us. "It has not yet been revealed what we shall be, but we know that when He is revealed, we shall be like Him; for we shall see Him as He is" (1 John 3:2).

"And so it is written: 'The first man Adam became a living being.' The last Adam became a life-giving spirit. However, the spiritual is not first, but the natural, and afterward the spiritual. The first man was of the earth, made of dust; the second Man is the Lord from heaven. As was the man of dust, so also are those who are made of dust; and as is the heavenly Man, so also are those who are heavenly. And as we have borne the image of the man of dust, we shall also bear the image of the heavenly Man" (1 Corinthians 15:45–49).

It is interesting to see that this process, which was begun in Genesis, is declared to be completed in Revelation, where the "one like the Son of man" gave John this significant message to the overcomers: "He who overcomes, I will make him a pillar in the temple of My God, and he shall go out no more. I will write on him the name of My God and the name of the city of My God, the New Jerusalem, which comes down out of heaven from My God. And I will write on him My new name" (Revelation 3:12). Since name always means character in the Bible, this message can only mean that at last God's purpose is accomplished—man has been so made into what God intended from the first,

His likeness and image, that he merits having the name of God written on him!

Words fail before such a glorious destiny as this! But our Lord foreshadows it in His wonderful prayer when He asks for His brethren that "they all may be one, as You, Father, are in Me, and I in You; that they also may be one in Us, that the world may believe that You sent Me. And the glory which You gave Me I have given them, that they may be one just as We are one: I in them, and You in Me; that they may be made perfect in one" (John 17:21–23).

Paul also foreshadows this glorious consummation when he declares that if we suffer with Christ we will also be glorified with Him, and that the "sufferings of this present time are not worthy to be compared with the glory which shall be revealed in us" (Romans 8:18). The whole creation waits for the revealing of this glory, for the "earnest expectation of the creation eagerly waits for the revealing of the sons of God" (Romans 8:19). And he adds finally: "Not only that, but we also who have the firstfruits of the Spirit, even we ourselves groan within ourselves, eagerly waiting for the adoption, the redemption of our body" (Romans 8:23).

In view of such a glorious destiny, shall we not cheerfully welcome the processes, however painful they may be, by which we are to reach it? And shall we not strive eagerly and earnestly to be "laborers together with God" in helping to bring it about? He is the great master Builder, but He wants our cooperation in building up the fabric of our characters, and He exhorts us to be careful how we build. All of us at every moment of our lives are engaged in this building. Sometimes we build with gold, silver, and precious stones, and sometimes we build with wood, hay, and stubble (see 1 Corinthians 3:12). And we are solemnly warned that every man's work is going to be revealed, "for the Day will declare it, because it will be revealed by fire" (1 Corinthians 3:13).

To my mind there is no more solemn passage in the whole Bible than the one in Galatians that says: "Do not be deceived, God is not mocked; for whatever a man sows, that he will also reap. For he who sows to his flesh will of the flesh reap corruption, but he who sows to the Spirit will of the Spirit reap everlasting life" (Galatians 6:7–8). It is the awful inevitableness of this that is so awe-inspiring. It is far worse than any arbitrary punishment; for punishment can sometimes be averted, but there is no possibility of altering the working of a natural law such as this.

In order to be laborers with God, we must build not only with His materials but also by His processes. Our idea of building is of hard work done in the sweat of our brow, but God's idea is far different. Paul tells us what it is. "We all," he says, "with unveiled face, beholding as in a mirror the glory of the Lord, are being transformed into the same image from glory to glory, just as by the Spirit of the Lord" (2 Corinthians 3:18). Our work is to "behold," and as we behold, the Lord effects the marvelous transformation, and we are changed into the same image by the Spirit of the Lord. This means, of course, to behold not in our earthly sense of merely looking at a thing, but in the divine sense of really seeing it.

Let me give an illustration. Someone offends me, and I am tempted to get angry and retaliate. But I look at Christ and think of what He would have done and dwell upon the thought of His gentleness and meekness and His love for the offending one. And as I look, I begin to want to be like Him, and I ask in faith that I may be made a "partaker of His nature." Anger and revenge die out of my heart, and I love my enemy and long to serve him.

It is by this sort of beholding Christ that we are to be changed into His image; and the nearer we keep to Him the more rapid the change will be.

If we would be conformed to the image of Christ, then we must live closer and closer to Him. We must become better and better acquainted with His character and His ways; we must look at things through His eyes and judge all things by His standards.

It is not by effort or by wrestling that this conformity is to be accomplished; it is by assimilation. According to a natural law, we grow like those with whom we associate, and the stronger character always exercises the controlling influence. And, as divine law is all one with natural law, only working in a higher sphere and with more unhindered power, it need not seem mysterious to us that we should become like Christ by a spiritual union with Him.

Christ is to "dwell in our hearts by faith," and He can dwell there in no other way. Paul, when he tells us that he was crucified with Christ, says: "It is no longer I who live, but Christ lives in me; and the life which I now live in the flesh I live by faith in the Son of God, who loved me and gave Himself for me" (Galatians 2:20).

"Christ lives in me"—this is the transforming secret. If Christ lives in me, His life must be revealed in my flesh, and I cannot fail to be changed from glory to glory into His image.

Our Lord's teaching about this is emphatic. "Abide in Me," He says, "and I in you. As the branch cannot bear fruit of itself, unless it abides in the vine, neither can you, unless you abide in me. I am the vine, you are the branches. He who abides in Me, and I in him, bears much fruit; for without Me you can do nothing" (John 15:4–5).

If we abide in Him, and He in us, we can no more help bringing forth fruit than can the branches of a flourishing vine. In the very nature of things the fruit must come.

But we cannot take the "old man" into Christ. We must put off the old man with his deeds before we can "put on the Lord Jesus Christ." And the apostle Paul, in writing to the Colossians, bases his exhortations to holiness of life on the fact that they had done this. "Do not lie to one another," he says, "since you have put off the old man with his deeds, and have put on the new man who is renewed in knowledge according to the image of Him who created him" (Colossians 3:9–10).

Sin must disappear at the incoming of Christ. The "old man" must be put off if the new man is to reign. But both the putting off and the putting on must be done by faith. There is no other way. We must move our personality, our ego, our will out of self and into Christ. We must reckon ourselves to be dead to self and alive only to God. "Reckon yourselves to be dead indeed to sin, but alive to God in Christ Jesus our Lord. . . . And do not present your members as instruments of unrighteousness to sin, but present yourselves to God as being alive from the dead, and your members as instruments of righteousness to God" (Romans 6:11, 13).

The same kind of reckoning of faith, which brings the forgiveness of sins within our grasp, brings also this union with Christ. To those who do not understand the law of faith, this will be a mystery, but to those who understand it, the law of faith works unerringly and produces results. No one can read the seventh chapter of Hebrews and fail to see that faith is an all-conquering force. It is the creative force of the universe, the higher law that controls all the lower laws beneath it; and what looks like a miracle is simply the working of this higher controlling law.

"By faith we understand that the worlds were framed by the word of God, so that the things which are seen were not made of things which are visible" (Hebrews 11:3). We are told that "He spoke, and it was done; He commanded, and it stood fast" (Psalm 33:9). And our Lord tells us that if we have faith we can do the same. "Jesus answered and said to them, 'Have faith in God. For assuredly, I say to you, whoever says to this mountain, "Be removed and be cast into the sea," and does not doubt in his heart, but believes that those things he says will be done, he will have whatever he says. Therefore I say to you, whatever things you ask when you pray, believe that you receive them, and you will have them" (Mark 11:22–25).

Faith calls those things that don't exist as though they do, and, in so calling them, brings them into being. Therefore, although we cannot see any tangible sign of change when by faith we put off the old man and by faith put on the new man, yet it has really been done, and faith has accomplished it. Those souls who abandon the self-life and give themselves up to the Lord to be fully possessed by Him find that He takes possession of their being and works there to will and to do of His good pleasure.

Paul prayed for the Ephesians that Christ might dwell in their hearts by faith (see Ephesians 3:17), and this is the whole secret of being conformed to His image. If Christ is dwelling in my heart I must necessarily be Christlike. I cannot be unkind, irritable, self-seeking, or dishonest; but His gentleness, sweetness, tender compassion, and loving submission to the will of His Father must be apparent in my daily walk and conversation.

We will not be fully changed into the image of Christ until He appears, but meanwhile, the life of Jesus is "revealed in our flesh." Is it revealed in ours? Are we so "conformed to the image" of Christ that men see in us a glimpse of Him? Is it obvious to all around us that we have been with Jesus?

Paul says we are to be "epistles of Christ," known and read of all men, "written not with ink but by the Spirit of the living God, not on tablets of stone but on tablets of flesh, that is, of the heart" (Ephesians 3:2–3). If every child of God would begin from this day forward to be an "epistle of Christ," living a truly Christlike life, it would not be a month before the churches would all be crowded with inquirers, coming in to see what was the religion that could so transform human nature into something divine. We must meet unbelievers with transformed lives.

It is very easy to have a church religion or a prayer meeting religion or a Christian-work religion, but it is altogether a different thing to have an everyday religion. To show godly character at home is one of the most vital parts of Christianity, but it is also one far too rare; and it is not at all an uncommon thing to find Christians who "do their righteousness" before outsiders "to be seen of men," but who fail miserably in showing Christlike character at home.

"And when you pray, you shall not be like the hypocrites. For they love to pray standing in the synagogues and on the corners of the streets, that they may be seen by men. Assuredly, I say to you, they have their reward" (Matthew 6:5). What we do to be seen of men is seen of men, and that is all there is to it.

There is no conformity to the image of Christ in this sort of righteousness. To bear every-day trials cheerfully and be patient under home provocations; to return good for evil and meet the frictions of daily life with sweetness and gentleness; to suffer long and be kind; to not envy or flaunt oneself; to not be puffed up or seek one's own; to not be easily provoked; to think no evil; bear all things, believe all things, hope all things, endure all things—this is what it means to be conformed to the image of Christ! Do we know anything of such righteousness as this?

If we want our loved ones to trust the Lord, volumes of talk about it will not be one-thousandth part as convincing to them as the sight of a little real trust on our own part in the time of need.

Some Christians seem to think that the fruits that the Bible calls for are some form of outward religious work, such as holding meetings, visiting the poor, running charitable institutions, and so forth. But the fact is that the Bible scarcely mentions these at all as fruits of the Spirit but declares that the fruit of the Spirit is love, joy, peace, long-suffering, gentleness, goodness, faith, meekness, temperance. A Christlike character must necessarily be the fruit of Christ's indwelling. Other things will no doubt be the outcome of this character; but first and foremost comes the character, or all the rest is but a hollow sham.

In order to become conformed to the image of Christ, we must be made "partakers of the divine nature." And where this is the case, that divine nature must reveal itself. Our tastes, wishes, and purposes will become like Christ's tastes, wishes, and purposes. We will change eyes with Him and see things as He sees them.

I can hear someone asking, "But do you really mean to say that, in order to be made partakers of the divine nature, we must cease from our own efforts entirely and must simply by faith put on Christ and let Him live in us and work in us to will and to do of His good pleasure? And do you believe He will then actually do it?"

To this I answer most emphatically, Yes, I mean just that. I mean that if we abandon ourselves entirely to Him, He comes to abide in us and is Himself our life. We must commit our whole lives to Him and by faith abandon ourselves to Him and abide in Him. By faith we must put off the old man and put on the new man. By faith we must consider ourselves dead to sin and alive to God. By faith we must realize that our daily life is Christ living in us, and we must allow Him to work in us to will and to do of His good pleasure. It is no longer truth about Him that must fill our hearts, but it is Himself, who will, if we let Him, make us His dwelling place, and who will reign and rule within us.

It was no mere figure of speech when our Lord in that wonderful Sermon on the Mount said to His disciples: "Therefore you shall be perfect, just as your Father in heaven is perfect" (Matthew 5:48). He meant, of course, according to our measure, but He meant that reality of being conformed to His image. And in Hebrews we are shown how it is to be brought about. "Now may the God of peace who brought up our Lord Jesus from the dead, that great Shepherd of the sheep, through the blood of the everlasting covenant, make you complete in every good work to do His will, working in you what is well pleasing in His sight, through Jesus Christ, to whom be glory forever and ever. Amen" (Hebrews 13:20–21).

It is to be by His working in us that this purpose of God in our creation is to be accomplished. If it should look like some of us are too far removed from any conformity to the image of Christ for such a transformation to ever happen, we must remember that our Maker is not finished making us yet. The day will come, if we do not hinder it, when the work begun in Genesis will be finished in Revelation.

12

GOD IS ENOUGH

My soul, wait silently for God alone, for my
expectation is from Him. He only is my rock and
my salvation; He is my defense; I shall not be
moved. In God is my salvation and my glory; the
rock of my strength, and my refuge, is in God.

PSALM 62:5–7

The last and greatest lesson that the soul has
to learn is the fact that God, and God alone,
is enough for all its needs. This is the lesson
that all His dealings with us are meant to
teach.

If God is indeed the "God of all comfort";
if He is our Shepherd; if He is really and truly

our Father; if, in short, all the many aspects we have been studying of His character and His ways are actually true, then we must come to the positive conviction that He is, in Himself alone, enough for all our possible needs, and that we may safely rest in Him absolutely and forever.

Most Christians have, I suppose, sung more often than they could count these words in one of our most familiar hymns: "Thou, O Christ, art all I want, more than all in Thee I find." But I doubt whether all of us could honestly say that the words have expressed any reality in our own experience. Christ has not been all we want. We have wanted a great many things besides Him. We have wanted fervent feelings about Him, or realizations of His presence with us, or an interior revelation of His love; or else we have demanded satisfactory schemes of doctrine, or successful Christian work, or something of one sort or another that will constitute a personal claim upon Him. Just Christ Himself, Christ alone, without the addition of any of our experiences concerning Him, has not been enough for us, and we do not even see how it is possible that He could be enough.

The psalmist said: "My soul, wait silently for God alone, for my expectation is from Him" (Psalm 62:5). But now the Christian says, "My soul, wait on my sound doctrines, for my expectation is from them"; or, "My soul, wait on my good feelings, or on my righteous works, or on my fervent prayers, or on my earnest striving, for my expectation is from these." To wait on God only seems one of the unsafest things they can do, and to have their expectation from Him alone is like building on the sand. They reach out on every side for something to depend on, and not until everything else fails will they put their trust in God alone.

No soul can be really at rest until it has given up all dependence on everything else and has been forced to depend on the Lord alone. As long as our expectation is from other things, nothing but disappointment awaits us. Feelings may change; doctrines and dogmas may be upset; Christian work may come to nothing; prayers may seem to lose their fervency; promises may seem to fail; everything that we have believed in or depended upon may seem to be swept away, and only God is left.

We say sometimes, "If I could only find a promise to fit my case, I could then be at rest." But promises may be misunderstood or misapplied, and, at the moment when we are leaning all our weight on them, they may seem utterly to fail us. But the Promiser, who is behind His promises, can never fail nor change. The little child does not need to have any promises from its mother to make it content; it has its mother herself, and she is enough. Its mother is better than a thousand promises. And should every promise be wiped out of the Bible, we would still have God left, and God would be enough.

I do not mean by this that we are not to have feelings or experiences or revelations or good works or sound doctrines. We may have all of these, but they must be the result of salvation and can never be depended upon as any indication of our spiritual condition. We are to hold ourselves absolutely independent of them all, resting in only the grand, magnificent fact that God is and that He is our Savior. We are to find God sufficient for all our spiritual needs, whether we feel ourselves to be in a desert or in a fertile valley. We are to say with the prophet: "Though the fig tree may not blossom, nor fruit be on the vines; though the labor of the olive may fail, and the fields yield no food; though the flock may be cut off from the fold, and there be no herd in the stalls—yet I will rejoice in the LORD, I will joy in the God of my salvation" (Habakkuk 3:17–18).

The soul can never find rest short of this. All God's dealings with us, therefore, are shaped to this end, and He is often obliged to deprive us of all joy in everything else in order that He may force us to find our joy only in Himself.

We have so accustomed ourselves to consider all the accompaniments of the spiritual life as being the spiritual life itself that it is hard to detach ourselves from them. We cannot think that the Lord can be anything to us unless we find in ourselves something to assure us of His love and His care. And when we talk about finding our all in Him, we generally mean that we find it in our feelings or our views about Him. If, for instance, we feel a glow of love toward Him, then we can say heartily that He is enough; but when this glow fails, then we no longer feel that we have found our all in Him. The truth is that what satisfies us is not the Lord, but our own feelings about the Lord. But we are not conscious of this; and consequently when our feelings fail we think it is the Lord who has failed.

Of course, all this is very foolish, but it is such a common experience that very few can see how foolish it is. Perhaps an illustration may help us to clearer vision. Let us think of a man accused of a crime, standing before a judge. Which would be the thing of moment for that man: his own feelings toward the judge or the judge's feelings toward him? Would he spend his time watching his own emotions and trying to see whether he felt that the judge was favorable to him or would he watch the judge and try to discover from his looks or his words whether or not to expect a favorable judgment? Of course we will say at once that the man's own feelings are not of the slightest account in the matter, and that only the opinions and feelings of the judge are worth a moment's thought. Upon the judge only would everything depend.

In the same way, if we will only bring our common sense to bear upon the subject, we cannot help seeing that the only vital thing in our relationship with the Lord is what His feelings are toward us.

This, then, is what I mean by God being enough. God is our answer to every question and every cry of need. If there is any lack in the One who has undertaken to save us, nothing supplementary we can do will avail to make it up; and if there is no lack in Him, then He Himself is enough.

The all-sufficiency of God ought to be as complete to the child of God as the all-sufficiency of a good mother is to the child of that mother. My own experience as a child taught me this. My mother was the remedy for all my ills and, I fully believed, for the ills of the whole world. And when anyone expressed doubts as to her capacity to remedy everything, I remembered with what fine scorn I used to annihilate them by saying, "Ah! But you don't know my mother."

And now, when any tempest-tossed soul fails to see that God is enough, I feel like saying, not with scorn, but with infinite pity, "Ah, dear friend, you do not know God! If you knew Him, you could not help seeing that He is the remedy for every need of your soul, and that He is an all-sufficient remedy. God is enough, even though no promise may seem to fit your case, nor any inward assurance give you confidence. The Promiser is more than His promises, and His existence is a surer ground of confidence than the most fervent inward feelings."

But someone may say, "All this is no doubt true, and I could easily believe it if I could only be sure it applied to me. But I am so good-for-nothing and so full of sin that I do not feel as if I had any claim to such riches of grace."

All the more, if you are good-for-nothing

and full of sin, have you a claim on the all-sufficiency of God. Your very good-for-nothingness and sinfulness are your loudest claims. The Bible declares that Christ Jesus came into the world to save sinners; not to save the righteous, not to save the fervent, not to save the earnest workers, but simply and only to save sinners.

If we want to see God, our interior questioning must be, not about ourselves, but about Him. How does God feel toward me? Is His love for me warm enough? Has He enough zeal? Does He feel my need deeply enough? Is He sufficiently in earnest? Although these questions may seem irreverent to some, they simply embody the doubts and fears of many doubting hearts, and they only need to be asked to prove the fact that these doubts and fears are in themselves the real irreverence. We all know what would be the triumphant answers to such questions. No doubts could withstand their testimony; and the soul that asks and answers them honestly will know the profound and absolute conviction that God is enough.

"All things are yours," declares the apostle Paul, "whether Paul or Apollos or Cephas, or the world or life or death, or things present or things to come—all are yours. And you are Christ's, and Christ is God's" (1 Corinthians 3:21–23). It would be impossible for any statement to be more all-embracing. All things are yours because you belong to Christ. All things we need are part of our inheritance in Him, and they only await our claiming. Let our needs and difficulties be as great as they may, there is in these "all things" a supply exceedingly abundantly above all we can ask or think.

Because He is, all must go right for us. While God lives, His children must be cared for. What else could He do, being what He is? He knows everything, He cares about everything, He can manage everything, and He loves us. What more could we ask?

Paul could say triumphantly in the midst of many trials: "For I am persuaded that neither death nor life, nor angels nor principalities nor powers, nor things present nor things to come, nor height nor depth, nor any other created thing, shall be able to separate us from the love of God which is in Christ Jesus our Lord" (Romans 8:38–39).

Nothing can separate you from God's love, absolutely nothing. Can we not understand that God, who is love, who is, if I may say so, made out of love, simply cannot help blessing us. We do not need to beg Him to bless us, He simply cannot help it.

Therefore God is enough! God is enough for time, God is enough for eternity. God is enough!